LONGMAN LITERATURE

Wide-Eyed and Legless

Jack Rosenthal

A play based on the true story by Deric Longden

Editors: Geoff Barton and Jane Christopher

Longman Literature
Series editor: Roy Blatchford

Plays

Alan Ayckbourn *Absurd Person Singular* 0 582 06020 6
Ad de Bont *Mirad, a Boy from Bosnia* 0 582 24949 X
Oliver Goldsmith *She Stoops to Conquer* 0 582 25397 7
Henrik Ibsen *Three Plays: The Wild Duck, Ghosts and A Doll's House* 0 582 24948 1
Ben Jonson *Volpone* 0 582 25408 6
Christopher Marlowe *Doctor Faustus* 0 582 25409 4
Arthur Miller *An Enemy of the People* 0 582 09717 7
J B Priestley *An Inspector Calls* 0 582 06012 5
Terence Rattigan *The Winslow Boy* 0 582 06019 2
Jack Rosenthal *Wide-Eyed and Legless* 0 582 24950 3
Willy Russell *Educating Rita* 0 582 06013 3
  Shirley Valentine 0 582 08173 4
Peter Shaffer *Equus* 0 582 09712 6
  The Royal Hunt of the Sun 0 582 06014 1
Bernard Shaw *Arms and the Man* 0 582 07785 0
  The Devil's Disciple 0 582 25410 8
  Pygmalion 0 582 06015 X
  Saint Joan 0 582 07786 9
R B Sheridan *The Rivals* and *The School for Scandal* 0 582 25396 9
Oscar Wilde *The Importance of Being Earnest* 0 582 07784 2

Longman Literature Shakespeare
Series editor: Roy Blatchford

A Midsummer Night's Dream 0 582 08833 X (paper)
  0 582 24590 7 (cased)
As You Like It 0 582 23661 4 (paper)
Hamlet 0 582 09720 7 (paper)
Henry IV Part I 0 582 23660 6 (paper)
Henry V 0 582 22584 1 (paper)
Julius Caesar 0 582 08828 3 (paper)
  0 582 24589 3 (cased)
King Lear 0 582 09718 5 (paper)
Macbeth 0 582 08827 5 (paper)
  0 582 24592 3 (cased)
The Merchant of Venice 0 582 08835 6 (paper)
  0 582 24593 1 (cased)
Othello 0 582 09719 3 (paper)
Richard III 0 582 23663 0 (paper)
Romeo and Juliet 0 582 08836 4 (paper)
  0 582 24591 5 (cased)
The Tempest 0 582 22583 3 (paper)
Twelfth Night 0 582 08834 8 (paper)

Other titles in the Longman Literature series are listed on page 113.

Contents

The writer on writing   v

    Starting to write   v
    Diana's illness   vi
    A writing routine   viii
    Diana's death   ix
    Diana's story   x
    A balanced tone   xii
    Final scenes   xii
    Involvement of Jack Rosenthal   xiii

Introduction   xvi

    Comedy and tragedy   xvi
    Myalgic Encephalomyelitis (ME)   xvii
    Human drama   xviii
    From prose to drama   xix
    Reading the screenplay   xxi

Reading log   xxii

Wide-Eyed and Legless   1

Glossary: reading the text   92

Study programme   98

    Characters   98
    Themes   104
    Structure and language   107
    Study questions   108
    Suggestions for further reading   111
    Wider reading assignments   112

The writer on writing

by Deric Longden

Starting to write

In 1974 BBC Radio Derby ran a short story competition. Each entry had to be submitted under a pen name and so I called myself 'Biro'.

My story was about a hundred-year-old man who put his great age down to the fact that he had always lived in a house with an outside toilet.

It kept you on your toes, he said. There was no easy trot upstairs when you had to go to the lavvy, not like when you have one inside. You never quite knew when you might have to sprint thirty yards up the garden path in the pouring rain, with the key in one hand and the ***Daily Mirror*** in the other.

Somehow I won and the following year I entered again, this time under the pen name 'Bic'. I wrote a story about a shepherd who only had two sheep and so he took them home with him every evening, rather than leave them out on the lonely moors at night.

Most shepherds dip their sheep once a year, but he was able to dip his once a week because fortunately he had a double draining sink unit. Then he would pop them into the tumble-dryer – for forty minutes on woollens.

I won again and the following year I went for the hat-trick. A week after I had posted my entry the producer rang me.

Are you Papermate?' I said I was and he told me that I looked like winning once again. 'If you withdraw,' he said, 'we'll give you a regular slot.'

Two and a half thousand broadcasts later I wince slightly when I look at the stories now. Although, if I am honest with myself, I smile as I wince.

They were original. They were me. And that it is the most powerful weapon we have in our armoury. There is nobody in the world quite like you and there is nobody in the world quite like me.

Diana's illness

It was the writing that helped to keep me sane during Diana's long illness. We had been married for twelve years when a mysterious virus struck her down. We had two lovely children and two new cars in the garage – she had two shops and I had two lives; one as a ladies' lingerie manufacturer and the other as a would-be writer.

Six months later she was in a permanent state of exhaustion. She would crawl out of bed in the morning, get dressed, and the effort would take so much out of her that she would have to crawl back in between the sheets for the rest of the day.

Then her hands began to claw. Something – God knows what – made her fingers twist until the nails were biting deep into the palms of her hands and then they would have to be forcibly straightened, often until they broke and had to be reset.

Before long her toes came out in sympathy and her arms began to roll back on themselves. It was as though every sinew in her body had been shortened by some two inches.

She wore plaster casts on her hands, with swooping wire cages to hold her fingers in position, but when an attack began its onslaught then the plaster would crack and the wire would buckle and all I could do was to love her and watch as her fingers clawed and the pain twisted her lovely face. This was to be the pattern of her life for the next fifteen years.

I could never guarantee to be anywhere on time and it wasn't long before my business began to run downhill and so I had to make a decision. I needed to be at home, looking after her. I could do it with love, whereas a nurse would do it with Valium. But the big question was — could I earn a living from writing?

The odds were against it. Radio doesn't pay very well and local radio pays hardly anything at all and so I had to go for quantity. I wrote thousands of short pieces, episodes for serials, jokes for comedians, the odd play. It was like being on the Ford production line. I wrote during the night, throughout the night, before breakfast and after a fashion.

During the winter months I also became a football commentator, selling match reports to the evening and Sunday newspapers. Waste not — want not. Once, when a game was abandoned because of a waterlogged pitch, I interviewed a small duck who just happened to be swimming in the penalty area. I couldn't afford not to get paid — I had to have something.

The duck turned out to be far more entertaining than most football managers. Every time I asked him a question he would rise to the challenge and quack knowingly. As far as he was concerned six inches of standing water would have made for a much more interesting game. The radio station played the tape seven times during the afternoon — it was different.

My kids were wonderful and gladly filled in for me on those rare occasions when I had to leave the house. They grew up quickly from the very first moment Diana fell ill.

I wrote on an ironing-board in the bathroom. An ironing-board makes a great desk. You have a padded surface for the typewriter, a heat-proof stand for a mug of tea at one end and there's plenty of room for an ashtray and a packet of cigarettes at the other. The rack underneath will take several reference books and the whole is easily portable.

I used to sit on the edge of the bath, breaking off only to go and check up on Diana, or so that either Nick or Sally could come in to use the toilet, or perhaps rinse out the odd bra in the sink – Sally that is, not Nick.

A writing routine

What developed from this frantic regime, apart from a weight loss of some three stones and an ulcer, was a writing style that was mine alone.

It grew out of a bizarre mixture of pain and sorrow, of realising what was important in life and of a driving need to wrap the all too obvious truth in a cocoon of wierd reality and gentle humour.

The truth was that Diana wasn't going to get any better. She could only get worse – and then what?

As she needed more and more of my time I had to cut down on my workload and so I began to refine and rework some of my earlier material and then I went after the more lucrative markets.

Radio 4 was an obvious target – they deal heavily in the spoken word. And then there were the women's magazines. Men's magazines tend to be more specialised, either that or they are up there on the top shelf in the newsagents.

I found that my daily routine of caring, cooking, shopping and housework, mixed in with a regular dose of hospital visiting gave me an insight into a woman's world that is denied to most men.

I became a regular on **Woman's Hour**. They needed a series of four and a half minute humour spots and I seemed to fit the bill. The staff at Radio Derby allowed me plenty of studio time, mainly at night, so that I could record the pieces – out of the kindness of their hearts and a deep embarrassment at having grossly underpaid me all these years.

I owe a lot to Radio Derby. I was allowed to make mistakes there, to learn the craft and experiment at strange hours when only a handful of hardy faithfuls would be listening. Without them nothing would have happened for me and I shall always be grateful.

Diana's death

And then Diana died. I won't go into the details here – I've lived through that moment over and over again, every day for the past ten years and it has torn me to pieces.

Let's just say that I found her drowned in the bath early one morning, just the thickness of the floorboards separating us as I wrestled with a reluctant washing machine down in the kitchen below.

The guilt was horrendous. I should have been with her – should have been keeping an eye on her. She had always been far too adventurous for her own good and now I had failed her when she needed me most.

The funeral arrangements, the funeral itself and the selling of a house in which I could no longer bear to live, burned up the hours immediately after her death and then – and then what? A friend of ours, the novelist Aileen Armitage, had moved into a spacious new flat in Huddersfield. There was room there for me, she said, and Sally too if she wished, while we sorted out our lives.

It was a wonderful old house that believed in itself. There was a certain peace about the place that wrapped itself around you the moment you walked in through the front door – a peace that had much to do with Aileen's calm and gentle presence.

And so we moved in and in a sense I took Diana with me too. She had been ripped out of my life without so much as a by-your-leave and I had never had the chance to say goodbye. I had only the memories...

And so I wrote about Diana, about our life together, all day, most days – short pieces each lasting about four and a half minutes. That's what I had been training myself to do all these years. I had become the champion of the one yard sprint.

In a room close by Aileen would be hard at work on her latest novel. She already had twenty or so titles to her credit. She would start in January on page one and by December, some five hundred pages later, she would be pulling the threads of the story together, ready to type – the end.

I couldn't possibly do that. She was a marathon runner – I was a sprinter. The thought of all those blank pages stretching ahead, waiting to be filled – with what? With the lives of two rather ordinary people, that's what.

Diana's story

I sent the short pieces off to June Hall, the literary agent, and she invited me to come down and see her in London. Now there are agents and there are agents – I was lucky, I got June Hall.

'It needs to be a book,' she said and I wilted slightly. She waved her hand over my short stories. 'They are very funny.'

I positively bloomed.

'But where's the pain?' she asked. And with my tail between my legs and my short stories clutched in my hot little hand, I set off back to Huddersfield, on a long voyage into the unknown – to write the pain.

It was something I had always avoided on the radio. Can't go depressing the listeners – not halfway through the afternoon you can't. The off switch is too handy and so Diana had been in a wheelchair yes, and sometimes in hospital, but in pain – never.

I began to tackle it. It wasn't easy and I failed miserably – until, almost without knowing, I began to write for myself rather than for other people. And then the shackles were off and I began to experience that tingle that comes only when you know that you are getting something right.

I still had a big problem with those three hundred or so empty pages stretching out ahead of me, and then one day I picked up a newspaper and saw the Olympic flag – five simple rings all linked together.

Then I had it. Each ring would equal one of my four and a half minute pieces and then, instead of reaching out for a conclusion at the top of page three, the story would slide smoothly into the next.

I knew I could write one ring – I had been doing it for years. Five interconnecting rings would give me a whole chapter and in no time at all I was off and running.

To be honest I hardly thought of my Olympic flag after that, but it had done the trick. Instead of seeing this impossible mountain looming ahead of me, I now bounded up the lower slopes, one at a time, and after a week or so I was amazed at how far I had climbed.

Perhaps bounding is the wrong word. Nowadays I am a very slow writer. I once read somewhere that William Horwood wrote the final 29,000 words of **Duncton Wood** in ten days. Almost 3,000 words a day. I stabbed at my spell-check immediately and counted my previous day's output – 43 words.

In fact I'm not all that keen on writing. I love re-writing. Once I've got the painful business over, that of drafting out the original story, then I could tinker with it for ever – like a motor mechanic with a classic car.

A balanced tone

I had thought that attaining a balance between the sadness and the humour of our situation was going to take more than a little tinkering. But I needn't have worried. I was writing about real life and in real life sadness and humour go hand-in-hand. They massage one another. The humour in the TV comedy **Steptoe and Son** arose quite naturally out of a very sad situation. It doesn't work the other way around. If we lived life in the average TV sit-com we would go mad within a week.

Diana had a wonderfully wry sense of humour – it would have gone down well in the trenches during the First World War. The worse things became for us, the more raw material she seemed to find.

There were times, however, when Diana was so very ill and our situation so dire that I thought I might test the reader's staying power and so at that point I would bring my mother into the story.

My mother had a sort of a ley line running through her brain. Logic went in one side and then got itself ever so slightly twisted before it came bubbling out of the other.

'You know, Deric, ten minutes of this rain will do more good in half an hour than a fortnight of ordinary rain would do in a month.'

She never had the slightest idea that she was being funny. All her lines sprang straight from her warm and loving soul. Jokes would have been totally out of place – a weak acknowledgment that the story needed lightening. But my mother's character was so genuine that I was able to fold her right into the heart of the story.

Final scenes

The final scenes, in the bathroom and at the funeral, seemed to take an eternity to write and then the book was finished.

BBC producer, Pat McLoughlin, accepted it for **Woman's Hour** and whittled it down so that it ran to eleven episodes. A radio abridgement can often amount to little more than butchery, but Pat completed the task with such skill that the book looked as though it had merely gone on a diet and lost a few pounds.

Within a week it was in **The Sunday Times** top ten bestsellers list, had been abridged in **The Reader's Digest** and won a special prize at the NCR book awards. Since then it has been published all over Europe, although at the moment the Americans consider it to be a little 'too English'.

Involvement of Jack Rosenthal

However, that could change any day now. I suppose all authors feel that their book, above all others, would make a wonderful film. I certainly did and I looked forward to a weekend in Essex where I was to address a writer's conference along with Jack Rosenthal and his wife, Maureen Lipman.

Jack had long been a hero of mine. His television plays **Bar Mitzvah Boy** and **The Evacuees** were both in my video collection and had also stood for years, well thumbed, on my bookshelves. I had followed his work from the early days of **Coronation Street** and still feel that his plays **Another Sunday and Sweet FA** and **The Knowledge** were perhaps the best two reasons ever for owning a television set.

I desperately wanted Jack to read my book, to tell me it was brilliant and that he was going home immediately to write the sceenplay. But I knew he had a heavy workload and was not a great reader of other people's books. As it turned out his misfortune was my good fortune. He had to go into hospital for an operation and Maureen made sure that **Diana's Story** was by his bedside when he came round.

He rang me a few days later and within a week or so had begun work on the screenplay.

Jack's method of adapting a book for the screen, and I do hope I have this right, is to get rid of everything in the story he can do without. This leaves him with that which he can't do without – and there he has the heart of the screenplay. Having established the main storyline he can then reassess the discarded material and use it to flesh out the characters.

He was extremely considerate throughout, sending me the first draft and each of the subsequent drafts. We talked long and often, agreed a lot and argued a little and then it was time to go in search of a production company.

Island World had just been formed by Tony Garnett and Margaret Mathieson and their timing couldn't have been better as far as we were concerned. Both had formidable reputations in the business and **Wide-Eyed and Legless** was to be their first venture with the new company, which has since gone from success to success – the television series **Cardiac Arrest** and **Between The Lines** immediately spring to mind.

The casting was perhaps the weirdest part of the whole process. Who would you like to see playing the part of yourself in a film? It's easy to be flip about these things – I always told people that I wanted Arnold Schwarzenegger, but in reality I hadn't the faintest idea.

Julie Walters was born to play Diana, Sian Thomas made a wonderful Aileen and my mother just couldn't have been anyone other than Thora Hird – but what about me?

Director Richard Loncraine went for Jim Broadbent and it turned out to be an inspired choice. He looks nothing like me, but he caught all the feelings, all the emotions and now I couldn't think of anyone else playing the part.

The play was a great success on British television, winning two BAFTA nominations for best film and best actress, and now it has been released as a full-blown movie in America, weirdly retitled **The Wedding Gift**. It opened in Los Angeles and New York to some extremely good reviews and right now I am keeping my fingers crossed.

Whatever happens, the most wonderful thing of all is that Diana, who was extremely talented but who could only sit by and watch as it was drained away from her by years of pain and frustration, is now known and loved the world over.

It doesn't make up for her suffering – but it's something.

September 1994

Introduction

Comedy and tragedy

When you have finished reading or performing **Wide-Eyed and Legless** you might find yourself wondering what kind of work it is. It seems to contain so many unusual and contrasting ingredients. Firstly, it is a television film based on a book, with characters based on real-life people. Then it is a tragedy – the story of one woman's fight against a disease that no one can explain – and yet it is full of comic situations and very funny one-liners. It contains death, and yet celebrates life.

In other words, this is no simple screenplay.

Perhaps the most important of these elements is the contrast between its subject-matter (the storyline) and its tone (the way the story is told). Summarised starkly, the storyline could seem grim and dispiriting. But whilst it portrays moments of real sadness and distress, the final effect is uplifting rather than depressing. It powerfully shows us the human spirit to fight on, and this seems by the end so much more important than the account of Diana's disease.

Diana Longden battles against a condition which neither she nor her husband Deric understand, and which the medical profession is unable to explain. Like so many human beings faced with what cannot be explained, they retreat into what they know best – their relationship, their family, their routines and their sense of humour. Together, these features of their lives provide them with a way of coping with an illness which, at the time, was almost unheard of.

Myalgic Encephalomyelitis (ME)

Myalgic Encephalomyelitis, or ME, is also known as Post Viral Fatigue Syndrome (PVFS) and Chronic Fatigue and Immune Dysfunction Syndrome (CFIDS). ME is a disease that affects over 150,000 people in the United Kingdom and, although it rarely kills, it ruins the lives of those who suffer from it. Fit, hard-working people aged 25–35 are most commonly affected, but it can and does also affect young and old alike, with an increase in cases in the under 11 age group.

The symptoms of ME can include headaches, memory and speech problems, muscle fatigue and exhaustion, pain throughout the body, particularly in the muscles, nausea, shivering, diarrhoea, digestive problems and sleeping at the wrong time – especially during the day and being wide awake at night.

All of these symptoms can be extreme and are adversely affected by any physical or mental exertion. The organisation *Action for ME* describes the feeling of this disease as a mixture of having flu, a hangover and just having run five miles. This should help you to understand why a short walk to the local shop can cause an ME sufferer to be bedridden, exhausted and experience blinding headaches, muscle pain and nausea. In **Wide-Eyed and Legless**, this is all too apparent when an afternoon spent looking around the shops in her wheelchair, pushed by Deric, forces Diana to spend a week recuperating in bed.

The most recent research into ME suggests that it is a result of immune system dysfunction (the body's protection system not working). However some researchers believe that it is derived from a persistent viral infection, with most people recovering from flu-like symptoms and a minority developing ME.

The point is that we are still not sure exactly what causes ME. Doctors now recognise that it is usually triggered by a viral infection but can also be triggered by other stresses such as: immunisation, antibiotics, life trauma and accidents.

INTRODUCTION

The variety of tests carried out on Diana and the reaction of the medical profession, indicate how little is known about this debilitating disease.

In **Wide-Eyed and Legless**, doctors, at a loss to explain Diana's symptoms, declare that she is suffering from 'Hysteria' – in other words that she is causing the illness herself; it is psychosomatic (caused by the mind). Deric is asked, 'How are her periods?' and Diana is told to watch her diet. Gradually, the fire of their curiosity is burnt out and she is left with precious little hope of even finding a name for her illness and instead only excruciating pain to remind her that it is not all in her mind. For this reason Diana has to fight ignorance and blindness as well as her disease in the play.

Human drama

This is what drama is best at – taking difficult subject matter which, in other forms, might prove too abstract or too remote from our own experience, and then showing the human consequences. In fact, this is how drama began in Ancient Greece. An audience of onlookers was encouraged to watch the actions and decisions of a character on stage and to trace the effects. The word *drama* derives from the Greek word *dran* meaning 'to do'. In this way one important function of drama was to teach us something about ourselves, seeing our own lives mirrored in those of the characters on stage.

Even though we might have no personal experience of severe illness, what **Wide-Eyed and Legless** provides is a strong sense of the way in which ordinary people adapt to survive, even when the pressure becomes almost intolerable.

The role of Deric Longden is important in this respect. When he wrote his autobiographical account of his life with Diana, he called it **Diana's Story**. And yet it is also *his* story. His role – as a victim of the disease in a different way – provokes us to think how we might react in similar circumstances, if a disease like ME were to grip one of our family.

Deric, with his loyalty, his career, and his wider responsibilities to his mother and children shows us the importance of family members in supporting the victim of disease, a role which he expertly describes in 'The writer on writing' on page v.

From prose to drama

Jack Rosenthal's sceenplay is based on Deric Longden's accounts of his life with Diana, but we need to remember that the role of the dramatist is different from that of the novelist or autobiographer.

Here, for example, is the way in which Deric Longden, in **Diana's Story**, describes Diana's visit to Fred, the hospital technician, who builds plaster casts to help prevent her hands from curling up:

Diana's hands were clawed. Something – God knows what – made her fingers twist until the nails bit into her palm and then she would have them forcibly straightened, often until they broke and had to be reset. Fred's hands were designed to slow the process down.

Fred was in charge of the Plaster Theatre at the Hallamshire Hospital in Sheffield, and his creations were works of wonder. Diana had two sets for each hand. One had a plaster cast that covered the outer arm from just below the elbow to the knuckles. Then four great metal arches leapt out of the back of the hands and hovered above the fingers like the bridge over the River Kwai. From each arch there was suspended an elastic band with a little upside-down saddle to take a finger. This stretched her fingers as straight as they would go – the thumb had its own little plaster cast. Set two were perfect casts of her inner arm, wrist and palms, and carried on to take the weight of her fingers, which were lashed in place with Velcro.

Thanks to Fred and his loving expertise, they gave Diana comfort and cut down the visits to the breaker's yard, although eventually the force that

INTRODUCTION

twisted her fingers would triumph over Fred's wire and plaster and his creations would crack and crumble.

'Never mind – we can rebuild her,' Fred would tell me as he bent Diana's fingers into a new contraption. 'Always remember, love – this is going to hurt you a lot more than it hurts me.'

Diana's Story, pages 10–11

Notice how much information Deric Longden is able to provide. He describes Diana's hands in detail ('Diana's hands were clawed'); he tells us about Fred's role ('Fred's hands were designed to slow the process down'); he provides details which answer the questions who? where? what? why?; he can give a sense of Fred's character through dialogue; and he creates humorous comparisons ('like the bridge over the River Kwai').

Now look at the way Jack Rosenthal creates the scene in the screenplay. Directions at the beginning describe what the camera will show us:

In the Hand Clinic the plaster casts DIANA *was wearing are now lying on a table.* DIANA *is seated at it, being fitted with new 'hands' by the technician,* FRED. *He's bluff and amiable and, over the years, has become a friend.*

The new plaster casts are even bigger and uglier than the old. They fasten over her arms from elbow to knuckles, terminating in four metal arches to which her fingers are attached by elastic bands.

DERIC *watches, suffering the pain with her, as Fred forces her hands into the contraptions.*

FRED   I'll tell you summat, Diana.
DIANA   (*wincing*) Whoever these fit marries Prince Charming.
FRED   No.
DIANA   Go on, then.
FRED   This is going to hurt you more than it hurts me.
DIANA   Thanks, Fred.

Scene 3, page 5

Much more of the information has to be shown to us rather than told directly. The complicated contraption for Diana's hands is represented visually; Fred's character will be conveyed through his behaviour and words; all the humour of the scene remains, as well as the pain.

Reading the screenplay

A screenplay works differently from many other texts that you might read in class, including drama texts. Before you embark upon reading the text, it is important to realise what you are *not* reading: this is not the kind of script you would encounter for a stage-play.

With a stage-play we usually expect some of the following elements: an opening scene establishing setting and character; some event which propels the plot; characters' reactions to the event; then perhaps a change of scene. The storyline, in other words, is usually unravelled in a linear way, gradually building a sense of development and progression.

A screenplay can shift more fluidly than that, switching scenes within a second — certainly faster than could physically be achieved on the stage. Writers like Jack Rosenthal recognise the power of placing scenes side-by-side to tell a story, and the way in which rapid editing can create a narrative flow which would be impossible in stage drama.

The important thing, then, when reading the screenplay is to try to *visualise* the events and characters as strongly as possible. The story, characterisation and themes are created by much more than the characters' words on the page: the directions, the settings, and the way one scene fits with the next — all of these play their part in conveying meaning.

The main point when working on the text in class is to keep up the pace. To assist in this, one person might serve as the linking narrator throughout, treating those italicised directions as if they were voiced by another character. In this way the unfolding drama of the storyline, and the mood changes from comedy to pathos, will become clearer and the overall effect of the screenplay all the more moving.

Reading log

One of the easiest ways of keeping track of your reading is to keep a log book. This can be any exercise book or folder that you have to hand, but make sure you reserve it exclusively for reflecting on your reading, both at home and in school.

As you read the screenplay, stop from time to time and think back over what you have read.

- Is there anything that puzzles you? Note down some questions that you might want to research, discuss with your friends or ask a teacher. Also note any quotations which strike you as important or memorable.
- Does your reading remind you of anything else you have read, heard or seen on TV or the cinema? Jot down what it is and where the similarities lie.
- Have you had any experiences similar to those occurring in the screenplay? Do you find yourself identifying closely with one or more of the characters? Record this as accurately as you can.
- Do you find yourself really liking, or really loathing, any of the characters? What is it about them that makes you feel so strongly? Make notes that you can add to.
- Can you picture the locations and settings? Draw maps, plans, diagrams, drawings, in fact any doodle that helps you make sense of these things.
- Now and again try to predict what will happen next in the plot. Use what you already know of the playwright and the characters to help you do this. Later record how close you were and whether you were surprised at the outcome.
- Write down any feelings that you have about the play. Your reading log should help you to make sense of your own ideas alongside those of the writer.

Wide-Eyed and Legless

Characters

Deric Longden
Diana Longden
Hospital Receptionist
Fred, Hospital Technician
Nurse
Gerald
Gerald's Mother
Young Doctor
Postman
Nick Longden
Deric's Mother
Factory Girls: One - Five
Joan
Sheila
Karen
Chemist
Sally Longden
'Kenneth of Arabia'
Ward Sister

Minnie Bonsall
Doctor Roper
Waitress at Luncheon
Aileen Armitage
Mâitre d'
Guests: One, Two, Three
Shop Assistant
Elderly Man
Driver
Optician
Café Waitress
Doctor
Old Man on Train
Wedding Guest
Meths Drinker
Vat Men
Minister
Various Guests, Shoppers, Patients etc.

SCENE ONE

1 The Longdens' house – Matlock, Derbyshire

It is December 1984. In the bedroom DERIC *(early forties) is crouched before the dressing-table mirror. He is half-dressed in shirt, underpants and socks. His trousers are on the bed, waiting their turn. At the moment he's struggling to tie his tie at the right length, then re-tying it. Throughout he's talking loudly to his wife,* DIANA, *who is not in the room.*

DERIC   . . . I mean, look at it from the tie's point of view. Poor old soul. Stuck in a drawer with seven odd cufflinks . . .

In the bathroom we see nothing but steam. It drifts in slow, hynoptic swirls. We gradually make out the shapes of bath taps as they drip rhythmically into the water in the bath.

DERIC'S VOICE   . . . one mouldy sock and a dead nasal inhaler, unloved and unwanted. Then, all of a sudden, it gets yanked out and twisted round a scraggy neck . . .

Back in the bedroom DERIC, *as before, is tying his tie.*

DERIC   I mean, what sort of a life is that? Mind you, I suppose it's worse for a jockstrap. *(He cocks his ear.)* Diana? You're not laughing . . .

From the bathroom:

DERIC'S VOICE   I crack my best joke of the morning . . . best joke of the week . . . and you . . . *(suddenly tense)* Diana?

DIANA *is floating motionless under the soapy water, her hair flowing outwards on the surface.*

DERIC   Jesus!

1

DERIC *has grabbed her head from behind and pulled it out of the water. She's unconscious. He holds her head upright, behind her, massaging her neck. He speaks quietly, tensely.*

DERIC   Diana! Wake up, love.

She slowly regains consciousness. She's an attractive woman (though not right now) in her late thirties.

DERIC   If you don't wake up I'll knock you senseless! Diana!!

DIANA *opens her eyes.*

DIANA   *(still drifting)* You've done that joke before. And it wasn't funny then . . .

DERIC   *(a sharp breath of relief)* You okay?

DIANA   Was it a blackout, again?

DERIC   Having them in the bath's not too clever.

They kiss.

DIANA   Made a right pig's ear of your tie, haven't you?

Another crisis is over. Despite his grin, we feel that, emotionally, it's taken even more out of DERIC *than it has* DIANA. *She knows it has.*

2 Country road, Derbyshire – Day

A not-so-young Citroën Safari is driving through the countryside. Rolling fields on either side. We hear the car radio playing a popsong.

DIANA'S VOICE   I remember when this was all fields.

DERIC'S VOICE   I remember it when it was all buildings before it was all fields.

SCENE THREE

DERIC is driving, his tie still slightly skew-whiff. DIANA is in the passenger seat. She's looking out of her window at the scenery. Despite the banter (and soon the singing), there's an underlying tension, an anxiety each feels about the other.

DIANA   I remember it when it was all fields before it was all buildings before it was all fields.

DERIC   *(grins)* You win.

The radio programme starts the next record. It's Andy Fairweather-Lowe singing 'Wide-Eyed and Legless'.

DIANA   Hey! They're playing my song!

They sing along for a while (including the title line).
The Citroën leaves the open moors and drops down towards a small town in the valley.

DIANA   I'd like you to play this at my funeral.

DERIC   I don't trust you. You'd sit up and start singing.

DIANA   *(soberly)* D'you think many people'll come to it?

DERIC   Not with your voice.

3 Hallamshire Hospital waiting room

It's a few days before Christmas and the hospital is doing it's best to put on a festive face. A roomful of waiting PATIENTS . . . silent and long suffering. Some are waiting for injuries to be attended to; some have their heads or limbs in plaster casts; others are in wheelchairs, beside their exhausted and sometimes even feebler spouses. Others are children.

DERIC *wheels* DIANA *into the room. They head for the Reception Desk.*

RECEPTIONIST   *(not bothering to look up)* Name?

DIANA   Arnold Schwarzenegger.

The RECEPTIONIST *jerks her head up – and almost manages a smile.*

RECEPTIONIST   Oh, hello Mrs Longden. How are you keeping?

DIANA   Oh, terrific, thanks. As long as you've got your health.

RECEPTIONIST   *(unaware of the irony)* That's the spirit. *(checks her ledger)* Now . . . four appointments again . . . Neurological, Renal, Hand Clinic and Consultant. I'll give you a shout.

Head on one side, Diana peers across the desk at a bulbous medical case-history file among a row of them on a table.

DIANA   My file, Deric. On the 'Great Mysteries of Our Time' shelf.

The RECEPTIONIST *overhears and glances over her shoulder at the files, then back again, severely, at* DIANA.

RECEPTIONIST   Don't even ask, Mrs Longden. The answer's no.

DIANA   One quick peek.

RECEPTIONIST   Like it's always no.

DERIC   Just while we're waiting.

RECEPTIONIST   It's not hers, it's her consultant's.

DERIC   What's it doing with her name on then? Going to a fancy dress party?

DERIC *swivels the wheelchair away and manoeuvres it into a space among the others. He sits beside her.*

SCENE THREE

DERIC Tell you what. I'll nip behind her counter and expose myself – create a diversion, while you nick your file.

DIANA We'd need a bigger diversion than that, love.

DERIC Thanks.

They sit for a moment in resigned silence amid the waiting PATIENTS. *A small, sad smile between them.*

In the Hand Clinic the plaster casts DIANA *was wearing are now lying on a table.* DIANA *is seated at it, being fitted with new 'hands' by the technician,* FRED. *He's bluff and amiable and, over the years, has become a friend.*

The new plaster casts are even bigger and uglier than the old. They fasten over her arms from elbow to knuckles, terminating in four metal arches to which her fingers are attached by elastic bands.

DERIC *watches, suffering the pain with her, as* FRED *forces her hands into the contraptions.*

FRED I'll tell you summat, Diana.

DIANA *(wincing)* Whoever these fit marries Prince Charming.

FRED No.

DIANA Go on, then.

FRED This is going to hurt you more than it hurts me.

DIANA Thanks, Fred.

The Renal Unit. DIANA, *in her wheelchair, has blacked out again. A nurse is frantically – and ineffectually – slapping her face.*

NURSE *(panicking)* What's happened!!? All I did was a blood test and she –

DERIC *steps across the room, levers the* NURSE *to one side, jerks* DIANA*'s head upright and whispers urgently.*

5

DERIC   Diana! Wake up! 'Dallas' is coming on! Diana! *(to the* NURSE*)* She has them a lot. Diana!!

NURSE   *(scared)* What are they?

DERIC   You tell us.

DIANA *begins to regain consciousness. The* NURSE *gazes at* DERIC *in admiration.*

DIANA   Sorry, chuck. Did it again, did I?

NURSE   *(to* DERIC*)* Hey! Brilliant! *(beat)* P'raps it's with coming here. People sometimes get anxious.

DERIC   No, love. It takes her two days in bed to gather the strength to get here . . . And three days in bed to recover. She isn't anxious. This is her at her best.

He takes DIANA'S *hand, kisses her brow, and sits on his haunches beside her.*

DIANA   Who do I have to sleep with to get a cup of tea round here?

The lift. The illuminated indicator shows that the lift is travelling down from 'Neurology'. DERIC *is standing behind* DIANA *who is still in her wheelchair. There are three or four other passengers, including a* WOMAN *standing behind her small son,* GERALD, *who's in a wheelchair.*

No one speaks, Everyone looks everywhere but at each other. Except DIANA *and* GERALD, *that is, who sit facing each other in their chairs, staring each other out. Finally –*

GERALD   What's wrong with thee, then?

GERALD'S MOTHER   *(horrified)* Gerald! Behave!

DIANA   I'm having my hands mended.

GERALD   You don't have a wheelchair 'cos you've got funny hands.

GERALD'S MOTHER Gerald!

DIANA No, but I've got funny legs, as well.

GERALD *puts his head on one side and appraises them.*

GERALD They look all right to me.

DIANA *(fluttering her eyelashes)* Well, thank you, Gerald.

The lift lurches to a halt, the doors rattle open and they all squeeze out into the corridor.

In the hospital corridor, outside the lift, GERALD'S MOTHER *is a metre or so ahead of* DERIC *and* DIANA, *propelling* GERALD *along in his wheelchair.*

GERALD *(over his shoulder)* D'you want a race?

DIANA *(excited)* You're on! Last one to the fire bucket's a consultant!

DERIC *scoots* DIANA *along, chasing after* GERALD'S *wheelchair.*

GERALD *(delighted)* Faster, mam! Faster!

Just as the race is getting neck-and-neck, GERALD'S MOTHER *suddenly swerves him down a branch corridor. His face crumples.*

GERALD No, mam! Don't mam!

She ignores him. DERIC *and* DIANA *stop at the junction, watching them go. Tears of frustration prick in* DIANA'S *eyes, just as they do in* GERALD'S. *A deflated pause.*

DIANA We could've won. I coulda been a contender, Charlie. Now all I got is a one-way ticket to Palookaville. *(sighs)* Where now?

DERIC Consultant.

DIANA Palookaville, all right . . .

DERIC *turns the wheelchair round and they set off back down the corridor.*

The consulting room. Intercut between DIANA'S *bulging case-history file, held in a young doctor's hands, and* DERIC *and* DIANA, *across the room, looking from the file to each other, then to the* DOCTOR . . . *waiting for him to speak.*

The DOCTOR *seems oblivious to them, slouched against a filing cabinet while he flicks through the pages.* DERIC *and* DIANA *are seated (she in her wheelchair) by the opposite wall. After a few moments of being ignored,* DIANA *whispers . . .*

DIANA   How about I expose myself, while you nick it?

The DOCTOR *glances up, unsure whether someone spoke.*

DOCTOR   Be with you in a sec, Mr Longden.

A wry glance between the addressee and the ignored patient.

DOCTOR   Just skimming through it. I'm filling in for Mr Loftus today.

DIANA   *(thrown)* Are you sure Mr Loftus still works here?

The DOCTOR *looks up from the file to* DERIC.

DOCTOR   Oh, I'm sorry. What was that?

DERIC   It was my wife who spoke.

The DOCTOR *glances across at* DIANA, *then back to* DERIC.

DOCTOR   Uh-huh. And what did she say?

DERIC   *(to* DIANA*)* The medical gentleman who's never seen your file before would like to know what you said, love.

DIANA   Oh . . . only that I've been coming here every three months for three years, and it'd be nice to see a consultant just once – if only to prove they didn't all go down with the 'Titanic'.

The DOCTOR *is barely listening . . . still flicking bemusedly through the pages.*

DOCTOR   Uh, huh, good, good . . . *(beat)* Been seen by three hospitals, no less. This, and two in London.

DIANA   Three in London.

DERIC   P'raps I can save you a bit of time, doctor. Five years ago, Diana got the flu; what we thought was the flu. The flu got better – and she got worse. Then came the pain. First her arms, then her legs, then everywhere. Her hands bunched up into claws, her arms began to bend back on themselves, over her shoulders. Nothing can force them back. In a week or so, these cages'll buckle and split and snap under the strain. A bit like she does, doctor. We'd like to know why.

The DOCTOR *stares at him, totally lost.*

DIANA   They did a biopsy on me a few months back – just down this corridor. I walked in, they cut a slice of muscle from my leg – and I've never walked since. They said it was nothing to do with the biopsy. I said 'What's it to do with, then?' They said they didn't know. I said 'How do you know it wasn't the biopsy, then?'

DERIC   Every day, she's more paralysed, and more exhausted. She has more and more pain, and more and more blackouts. All we'd like to know is what's wrong with her. What is it?

DIANA   And what's it say in that file? You've had three years to find out! What do they all say it is?

A silence, apart from distant hospital sounds. The DOCTOR *snaps the file shut. He ponders . . . at a loss.* DERIC *and* DIANA *wait, exhausted and tense, for his reply.*

DOCTOR   *(flailing)* Right . . . Um . . . *(Straw-clutching – to* DERIC*)* Tell me . . . how are her periods?

An incredulous pause.

DIANA   *(stiffly – to* DERIC*)* Home time?

DERIC   Home time.

DERIC *wheels a livid* DIANA *out of the consulting room.*

DIANA   'How are her periods?'!!

DERIC   Forget it.

DIANA   Moron . . .

DERIC   You were supposed to say 'Forget what?'

DIANA   Idiot!

DERIC   You know – like you've forgotten it already . . Oh, take no notice.

Suddenly, DIANA *breaks away, wheeling herself, agonising though it is. She veers round a corner.*

DERIC   What are you do —? Diana! You'll do your hands in!

In the waiting room many of the PATIENTS *we saw previously – and some new ones – are still waiting.* DIANA *bursts through the doors in her wheelchair.* DERIC *races in.*

DIANA   Attention, please! If any of you ladies fancy a bit

on the quiet, there's a little dick down the corridor
going spare.

DIANA *doesn't wait for a reaction, she kicks open the exit door and disappears. Everyone stares, not knowing whether to laugh or blush.* DERIC *smiles and follows* DIANA.

4 The Longdens' house

Christmas Eve. The POSTMAN *is perusing with interest the envelopes he's delivering. The door opens and* DERIC *appears.*

DERIC   Why do you never stick them in the letterbox like other postman?

POSTMAN   Card . . . bit late, must've just got yours. *She* magazine, returning your manuscript. Another rejection, no doubt. Still . . . save you a bit on toilet paper. D'you get it? Another card . . . *(examines next envelope)* Invitation, I think . . . you can open them here, I don't mind. How's Diana?

DERIC   Oh, you know.

POSTMAN   Right.

A white Cortina hurtles down the street and screams to a stop at the kerb. NICK LONGDEN *(about 19 years old) clambers out, dragging an overnight bag with him.*

NICK   Morning, all.

DERIC   Nice weekend, Nick?

NICK *beams exaggeratedly.*

POSTMAN   He's had a nice weekend . . . *(reads postcard)* 'Greetings from Morecambe. Love, Nick and Joanne.' 'Joanne'? Went with the Henshaw's lass, did you?

NICK *(to postman)* It's all right, her mother knows. You don't have to go round and tell her.

POSTMAN Hang on. How's this got here before he has?

DERIC He posts them before he goes.

NICK *(to postman)* Lateral thinking.

POSTMAN *(lewdly)* Saves time at the weekend, does it lad?

NICK Why don't you go and get your leg bitten off, like a proper postman?

The bedroom/landing: DERIC *is dressing* DIANA *on the bed, tugging on her tights.* DIANA *is peering at the invitation the postman brought, now open on the bed with the rest of the mail.* NICK *is on the other side of the half-open door, allowing* DIANA *a little privacy, leaning against the wall, with a bowl of Weetabix.*

DERIC So what else did you do? No one sits in the pictures for two days and three nights . . .

NICK Um . . .

DIANA Ignore him, Nick. When we had dirty weekends, we didn't go to the pictures either.

With a final effort, DERIC *gets* DIANA'S *tights on her.*

DIANA *(to Deric)* Better at pulling them off, aren't you, love? My white blouse next and my grey skirt. Second drawer.

DERIC *produces the neatly folded clothes from the drawer.*

DIANA What's that?

DERIC What?

DIANA In the middle.

DERIC *pulls out a colourful bikini from between the clothes.*

DERIC That bikini you've never worn. *(a sad beat)* You bought it at Kendal's. Just before you took ill.

DIANA I'll give it a go in the bath one day. Crack on it's the Bahamas. *(breaks the mood)* This invitation. You should go, love. It's a literary lunch.

NICK *taps on the door.*

NICK I've an official announcement to make. Can I put my head round?

He does so. DERIC *and* DIANA *look at him, expectantly.*

NICK We're getting married.

A cheer of delighted approval from DERIC *and* DIANA.

DERIC Hey!! *(then suspiciously)* Not a rush job, is it?

The phone abruptly starts ringing, next to the bed.

NICK That'll be for me, I'm flogging the Buick. I'll take it downstairs.

He disappears back round the door and clatters downstairs.

DIANA When's the big day?

NICK'S VOICE We've not decided yet. We're just establishing the principle.

DERIC *and* DIANA *are amused – and impressed.* DIANA *grins.*

DIANA Wow! Can't be a rush job, then . . .

5 Telephone conversation intercut between Deric's mother's kitchen and the Longdens' hallway

Deric's mother's kitchen

DERIC'S MOTHER *holds the phone, waiting for an answer. She notices her cat poking its nose out of a roll-top bread-bin on the floor. Beside it is a bowl of pilchards.*

MOTHER   Whisky! Eat your breakfast. There's cats starving in India. *(the cat ignores her)* Oh, all right, then. You've twisted my arm.

She puts the phone down, picks up a bag of sugar from the work surface and goes over to the cat.

The Longdens' hallway/stairs

NICK *gallops down the stairs towards the phone ringing on the hall table. He grabs it.*

NICK   *(into phone)* Hello? . . . Hello? *(calling upstairs)* No one there. Must be Grandma . . .

Deric's mother's kitchen

MOTHER *is sprinkling sugar on the pilchards. From the phone we hear:*

NICK'S VOICE   *(from phone)* Hello? Hello?

MOTHER *looks towards the phone, puzzled. She tut tuts, goes over to it and picks it up.*

MOTHER   *(into phone)* Who is that calling, please?

The Longdens' hallway

DERIC *is coming down the stairs to join* NICK.

NICK   *(into phone)* Hi, Grandma.

Mother's kitchen

MOTHER   *(to cat)* It's your nephew. *(into phone)* Whisky asked for more sugar on his pilchards.

The Longdens' hallway

DERIC *takes the phone.* NICK *thankfully makes his escape.*

DERIC   *(into phone)* It's me now.

Mother's kitchen

MOTHER   *(to cat)* Now it's your brother. *(into phone)* Guess who's popped his clogs? Count Basie. Shows you, first Johnny Weissmuller and now Count Basie. It was on the news. I liked Count Basie. What did you want?

The Longdens' hallway

DERIC'S *used to this kind of conversation with his mother.*

DERIC   *(into phone)* Nothing. You rang me.

Mother's kitchen

MOTHER   *(into phone)* If it was to tell me you're going to the factory today, can you pick up my prescription at Doctor Shaw's and take it to a chemist for me?

The Longdens' hallway

DERIC   *(into phone)* I'm not going to the factory.

Mother's kitchen

MOTHER   *(into phone)* On your way back, then.

6 The Longdens' house

In the bedroom DIANA, *now dressed, is propped up on the bed painting her fingernails. This is a tortuously slow process – both hands will take her all day. Finishing just one fingernail exhausts her.* DERIC, *now also fully dressed, is seated on the bed, briefcase beside him, ticking off items on a handwritten list.*

DERIC (*outwardly at ease; inwardly weighed down*) So, all in hand . . . washing machine on, ironing when I get back, thermos flask and sandwiches by the bed, the world's thinnest turkey defrosting . . .

NICK'S VOICE See you later, folks.

DIANA 'Bye, love.

DERIC Hang on Nick, you're on my list. Could you pick up a couple of pounds of sprouts and a jar of pickled walnuts?

In the hallway NICK *is combing his hair at the hall mirror, on his way out.*

NICK We don't like pickled walnuts, no one ever eats them.

He opens the front door.

DERIC'S VOICE That's not the point.

In the bedroom.

DIANA It's Christmas. We don't like sprouts either.

NICK'S VOICE Right.

DERIC *and* DIANA *as before.* DERIC *gets up to go.*

DIANA (*soberly*) I hope it's soon. The wedding.

DERIC'S *face saddens in anticipation of her next thought.*

DIANA I want to be there, don't I?

DERIC Well, of course you'll be there!

A painful pause – painful for both of them.

DIANA I'll have to buy a hat. I haven't worn a hat since our honeymoon.

DERIC 'Hat'? I remember black suspenders.

DIANA *(laughs)* Go on – off to your factory.

He kisses her tenderly.

DERIC You'll stay in bed?

DIANA Promise. Unless I get an urge to climb on the roof and repoint the chimney.

He taps her on the nose, picks up his briefcase and starts for the door.

DIANA Deric? If I am there . . . I'm going to walk down the aisle. *(beat)* Aren't I?

They stare at each other, trying to imagine the impossible.

DERIC Course you are.

DIANA Crawling on your hands and knees counts as walking, doesn't it?

DERIC *(a tentative smile)* See you later.

He goes. As the front door bangs to, her defences – and her face – crumble slightly.

7 Industrial Estate, Chesterfield

The Citroën drives down a street of small factories and parks outside one of them which is signposted 'Longden Lingerie Ltd'. In contrast to the spruce-looking factories around it, this one is neglected and down-at-heel. Its paint is peeling. Weeds grow on the front steps.

DERIC *switches off the engine of his parked car and sits staring morosely ahead. This is the first time we've seen him alone, without having to pretend the confidence and cheerfulness he shows in public. Beneath that constant disguise, he's haunted. He's a man on the very brink of emotional and physical breakdown.*

He takes a pipe and tobacco from the glove compartment, lights it and rehearses looking self-assured and carefree in the driving mirror.

DERIC   Good morning, ladies!

It doesn't ring quite as true as he'd hoped. He tries again.

DERIC   Morning, girls!

And again.

DERIC   Morning!

He shakes his head in defeat . . . then sticks the pipe in his mouth at a jaunty angle and gets out of the car.

In the factory machinists' room a distorted speaker is spewing out a version of 'Rocking Around the Christmas Tree'. The interior of the factory is as bleak and rundown as the outside. Four girls sit at idle sewing machines; reading, drinking mugs of tea; and chatting. JOAN *and* SHEILA, *the two supervisors, are poring over a dismantled sewing machine; one above it, the other beneath.* DERIC *strides in.*

DERIC   *(as rehearsed)* Morning, ladies!

The girls erupt into a great cheer. He's puzzled.

DERIC   What've I done – and who to?

1ST GIRL   It's today!

DERIC   What is?

2ND/3RD GIRLS   Pay-day, Deric! And the Christmas bonus!

4TH GIRL   Forgotten, hadn't you, Deric?

DERIC   I know what day it is, Jennifer. I'm renowned for it . . . What do you think I've come in for? I'm on my way to the bank . . .

He doesn't fool the girls for a second, but they cheer nevertheless. He evades further discussion by going over to JOAN *and* SHEILA *at the dismantled machine.*

JOAN   Don't say 'Have we tried a vet?' It's got nothing to live for.

DERIC   Pop in the office a sec, Joan. You too, Sheila.

He starts for the office, calling to the girls, en route.

DERIC   Well, don't just sit there like you've sod all to do.

5TH GIRL   We have sod all to do!

DERIC   Do some hand-jiving. Clean the windows.

5TH GIRL   We've cleaned them.

DERIC   Well mucky them up again.

He goes into the office. JOAN *and* SHEILA *follow.*

DERIC'S *office is as depressing as the rest of the factory.* DERIC *slumps into a chair behind his desk. He notices that his desk-calendar is out of date. He rips off several pages, crumples them into a ball and plays with it.* JOAN *and* SHEILA *trundle in.*

DERIC   I thought we'd fifty dozen waist-slips on the go?

SHEILA   That was a fortnight ago, love.

DERIC   Was it?

JOAN   What are you smoking lad?

DERIC   'Three Nuns'.

JOAN   Well, I think one of them's just farted. Put it out, Deric. It never fools anyone, anyway.

A worried pause. DERIC *toys aimlessly, emptily with the paper ball.*

DERIC   I'll phone Henry Margolis in Manchester. He may want something for the January sales.

SHEILA   There's nowt to make it out of, even if he does.

DERIC   Isn't there?

SHEILA   We haven't enough stock to make a shoulder-strap.

JOAN   *(to DERIC)* You're never here to order it, sunbeam. If you're never here, how can you ever expect to . . . *(beat)* How is she, by the way?

DERIC   *(getting up)* I'd best get that machine fixed.

SHEILA   What for?

He sits down again.

JOAN   *(enough's enough)* Deric. This place is losing you two hundred a week. That's over ten thousand a year. It's in arrears to the Inland Revenue and Customs and Excise. It's running a bank overdraft of . . .

DERIC   Yes, well . . . No good being realistic Joan.

SHEILA   What about your magazine writing?

DERIC   I've got a couple in the pipeline that might . . . I haven't really heard back yet . . .

JOAN   Deric. They don't pay enough to keep Kojak in haircuts. *(indicates SHEILA)* That was her joke, not mine.

SHEILA   Ta.

DERIC   *(wryly, to both)* Ta.

A difficult pause.

SHEILA *(tentatively)* It can all be put right in one fell swoop. You know that.

DERIC *(curtly)* And you know me. Forget your fell swoop, Sheila.

JOAN It's your only option, lad! If you were here full time, you could pay someone to look after her full time!

SHEILA That's not just us talking. It's Mr Tillotson at the bank. Everybody.

JOAN It's the best for both of you. It's a question of priorities.

DERIC Exactly. I'll fix that machine, nip to the bank, then get straight back to her.

He starts to get up. JOAN *puts her hand on his shoulder and presses him down again.*

JOAN I'll go to the bank. Mr Tillotson's less likely to hit a woman. *(pushes the phone towards him)* You phone Mr Margolis in Manchester.

In the factory tool room DERIC *is searching among spare parts and junk on the shelves. The sixth girl machinist,* KAREN, *comes out of the ladies' toilet – and sees* DERIC *through the open door of the tool room opposite. She crosses the corridor.*

KAREN *leans against the door-jamb, watching* DERIC *rummaging through the shelves. She twiddles a sprig of mistletoe in one hand. This is a chance she's long been waiting for.*

KAREN Well, they can say what they like. In my book, you're a gentleman.

DERIC Oh, hello, Karen. *(beat)* What? What who says?

She advances into the room a little and leans against the shelves.

KAREN Nursing poor Mrs Longden day and night. Standing by her. I mean, it's an example to the youth of today, that, isn't it? I mean, it's unusual even if the wife's, you know, normal and can have a . . . well, normal, healthy married life, kind of thing. I respect that in a man, staying faithful and that, in spite of . . . I mean –

DERIC *picks up the spare part he's been looking for.*

DERIC I think a brick wall'd know what you mean, Karen. 'Scuse me, love.

He squeezes past her and into the corridor. KAREN *stands, swallowing her anger.*

KAREN *(to herself)* Poofter! *(calls after him)* The rotten bank shuts in ten rotten minutes, you know!

She chucks the mistletoe after DERIC.

8 Mother's kitchen

DERIC'S MOTHER *is reading the label on a potted plant – the leaves of which are dead and drooping. She's talking to the cat which is sitting in the sink, watching her.*

MOTHER *(reads)* 'Make sure the roots are healthy.'

She yanks the plant out of its soil and peers at its roots.

MOTHER Looks fit enough to me . . .

She rams the plant back in the soil.

MOTHER It's just the leaves that seem a bit off-colour. Don't know why. *(beat)* Still, you know what they say. You're nearer to God in a garden than you are anywhere where you're not in a garden.

The phone rings.

MOTHER   That'll be the phone.

She takes it, and answers:

MOTHER   *(into phone)* Directory Enquiries? What town?

9 Telephone conversation: intercut between the chemist's shop and Mother's kitchen

DERIC *is behind the counter, standing with the* CHEMIST *at the dispensary door, phone in hand.*

DERIC   *(into phone)* Mum? Me. These sleeping pills I've to get. Do you know what strength they are?

Mother's kitchen

MOTHER   *(into phone)* I know what colour. Yellow.

Chemist's shop

DERIC *turns to the* CHEMIST, *shakes his head.*

CHEMIST   May I?

DERIC   *(handing him the phone)* You'd make me a very happy man.

CHEMIST   *(into phone)* The doctor didn't write it on the prescription, you see, and he's not there now and I can't dispense them if I don't know the strength . . .

Mother's kitchen

MOTHER *uproots another pot-plant.*

MOTHER   *(into phone)* That's all right, dear. I never take them anyway.

Chemist's shop

The CHEMIST *turns to* DERIC *in some alarm.*

DERIC   Don't tell me. Nothing she says surprises me. I wouldn't like to break the tradition.

CHEMIST   *(into phone)* But according to my records . . . you've had sixty Soneral tablets a month for the last five years!

Mother's kitchen

MOTHER *rams the dead plant back into the soil.*

MOTHER   *(into phone)* Correct. Nellie Elliott sucks most of them. And Mrs Next-Door sometimes borrows a few if her sister's had a bad night with the chickens.

Chemist's shop

The CHEMIST *pales. He assumes his most authoritative manner.*

CHEMIST   *(into phone)* I can't let you have them, Mrs Longden. Not until it's sorted out with your doctor.

Mother's kitchen

MOTHER *is pouring the cat's milk on to the pot-plants.*

MOTHER   *(into phone)* You don't have to call me 'Mrs Longden', Deric. *(beat)* You don't sound like Deric. *(beat)* Are you an obscene phone call?

The CHEMIST *has hung up.*

10 Interior of Citroën

DERIC *is driving. His look of haunted anxiety has returned. Bright Christmas pop music plays on the car radio.*

There's a sudden ear-splitting blast of a car horn. A car is racing towards him. DERIC *realises he's driving on the wrong side of the road. He swerves away just in time, but immediately into the path of another car blasting its horn behind him. The other car squeezes past, its driver swearing at him through the window, as* DERIC *swerves on to the pavement.*

DERIC *sits, hunched, for a moment, breathing hard, trying to calm himself. He assumes his cheerful public persona.*

DERIC   Right. Okay. Everything's okay. No problem.

He steers carefully back into the road and slowly drives the last few metres to his house.

11 The Longdens' hallway/stairs

DERIC *comes in, closing the door behind him. He calls upstairs as he does so.*

DERIC   Only me, love. I don't suppose Henry Margolis phoned, did he?

DIANA'S VOICE   Don't panic – I'm all right.

The blood drains from DERIC'S *face. He races to the stairs.* DIANA *is jammed, spreadeagled, between the wall and the newel, halfway down the stairs.*

DIANA   I was trying my double-somersault with the triple back-flip. I got ten for content and none for execution. I think I've laddered my tights . . .

12 Hallamshire Hospital – Night

DIANA'S *bedspace is curtained off and illuminated only by the ward's night-lights. Christmas carols can be faintly heard in the background.*

As well as her arms, imprisoned in their plaster cages, DIANA'S *leg is bandaged and propped up. Despite this, she's managed to jam her bedside phone between her chin and collar bone. She's at her (as yet) lowest ebb, fighting back unwanted tears. Throughout the conversation, despite the words themselves, she grows increasingly emotional.*

DIANA   *(into phone)* Hello. Who's on duty tonight? . . . Can I have a word with John or Ian then please? *(pause)* Hello Ian. It's Diana. Yes that's right. No, nothing new, really . . . Except . . . well, I don't know how much more I can take . . . Well, correction, I do know how much. None. It's all right, I can't do anything. I wish I could *(pause)* I've nearly broken my back dialling your number. And I can't chuck myself under a 52 bus – it's a terrible bus service down this ward.

In the corridor NICK *is seated on a bench, struggling to keep awake, smoking a cigarette. After a moment, he hears footsteps coming up the stairs. Grateful for a diversion, he goes to the banister rail and leans on it, to see who's coming.*

It's his sister, SALLY, *an attractive girl of about 21. She's lugging a suitcase.*

NICK   Hi, Sis. Happy Whatsit, or not, as the case may be.

SALLY   Hi. How is the great banana?

NICK *meets* SALLY *and takes her suitcase.*

NICK   Three fractures, internal bruising, black eye and throwing up all the time.

SALLY   Jesus God!

NICK   How was the train?

SALLY   Christmas Eve! It would've been quicker by reindeer.

NICK   Dad'll be back in about an hour. We're taking it in shifts through the night.

SALLY   You skedaddle. Get a night's sleep, the pair of you. And no more than three tangerines in my stocking.

NICK   She's in the Stafford Cripps Ward.

SALLY   By hell, she must be bad.

She kisses him.

NICK   *(sniffing)* You don't wear perfume!

SALLY   Who says?

NICK   *(pause, grin)* Oh, I get it.

SALLY *heads off down the corridor towards the ward.* NICK *calls after her.*

NICK   What's he like?

SALLY   *(without looking back)* Tall, good looking, funny, shy, sincere, kind, well-read, athletic, charming . . .

SALLY *disappears through a set of swing doors towards the ward, still talking.* NICK *watches her go, smiles and heads off down the stairs with the suitcase.*

In her bedspace DIANA *is speaking into the phone, as before.*

DIANA   *(into phone)* . . . All I'm saying is – I did what you said the last time I phoned. Had second thoughts. Only trouble is now I've had third, fourth and fifth ones – and I'm back where I started, still thinking it'd be for the best. For everyone. *(pause)* I know they do . . . That's why it's for the best. It's wrong for one life to muck up three. Without me, they'd . . .

She hears SALLY'S *footsteps approaching, struggles to replace the phone – and fails.*

SALLY   *(entering)* Hello, great banana.

SALLY *replaces the phone for her.*

DIANA   Damn thing – I knocked it off trying to get my Lucozade . . . Hello, Sally. Well, here I am again . . .

SALLY   It's the boiled cod, isn't it? You can't keep away.

13 *Mother's house*

Christmas Day. A quiet suburban street. DERIC *is helping his mother into the Citroën. Getting in and out of car is not one of her strong points, and she is having a little difficulty. A man,* KENNETH, *passes by on the opposite pavement.*

KENNETH   Merry Christmas, Deric.

DERIC   *(turning)* Oh, hello, Kenneth.

KENNETH   *(to thighs and corset)* Merry Christmas, Mrs Longden.

MOTHER   *(in mid-slide)* And to you, Lawrence.

DERIC   It's not Lawrence, it's Kenneth.

MOTHER   I knew it was Someone of Arabia.

14 *Hallamshire Hospital*

DERIC *and his* MOTHER *are among others making their way to the various wards. They reach a knot of visitors kept waiting outside the closed doors of a ward by a dragon of a* WARD SISTER, *standing guard.* MOTHER *barges through, trailed by an embarrassed* DERIC.

WARD SISTER *(sternly)* The doctor's still doing his rounds.

MOTHER S'alright, chuck, he won't get in my way.

MOTHER *sweeps down the ward past the patients in their beds.* DERIC *apologetically follows.*

MOTHER *waves at* DIANA, *in bed further down the ward. An elderly patient, in bed somewhere between mother and* DIANA, *waves back at her. This is* MINNIE. *She's knitting, wearing a paper hat.*

MINNIE Annie!

MOTHER *stops and peers at her. A slow smile of recognition.*

MOTHER Minnie Bonsall!

She goes over to her bedside.

MOTHER It must be fifteen years . . .

MINNIE Eighteen. Arthur's been dead eighteen years this week. It was at the funeral.

MOTHER That's right. *(sits on chair by the bed)* How is Arthur?

MINNIE Still dead.

MOTHER Oh, yes, he would be, wouldn't he? He never was one for change. *(beat)* Richard Burton popped his clogs last week. First James Mason, and now him. If it isn't someone, it's someone else.

DERIC *is now seated at* DIANA'S *bed.* DIANA *looks drawn.*

DIANA They've done more tests.

DERIC And?

DIANA I'm beginning to feel sorry for them. Sally asleep?

DERIC With all her old teddy bears. They're coming over after lunch, like you said, with the pickled walnuts.

DIANA She's become a croupier, you know?

DERIC Yeah.

DIANA I always thought she was a beauty therapist.

DERIC Me, too.

DIANA I think she's in love. At last.

DERIC She keeps smiling at herself in the mirror.

DIANA He's a croupier, too.

DERIC I know.

DIANA And a karate expert.

DERIC Oh, I didn't know that.

A pause. They smile at each other. Then her smile falters.

DIANA You look like I feel, love.

DERIC I've got no make-up on yet, that's all.

A pause.

DIANA The nurse said they're not bothering with any more tests. There's no more been invented . . .

MOTHER *comes wandering over to them, sits by the bed and takes* DIANA'S *hand.*

MOTHER How are you, love? Happy Christmas.

DIANA Oh, fine. Thanks for coming.

MOTHER Don't be silly – it's company for me. I'd brought you some ginger ale, but I've given it to

Minnie Bonsall – I don't think she's quite with us, she's knitting a dishcloth.

15 *Country road on hills above town*

The Citroën climbs the hill towards the open moors. DERIC *is driving home from the hospital.* MOTHER *is in the passenger seat. She seems remote, deep in thought.*

MOTHER You want to keep your eye on that girl. I've a feeling her fall did more damage than they think. She was sitting up peculiar. But more than that – it was her eyes. Her eyes tell you more than she does. *(beat)* Or is it just me being silly?

16 *Hallamshire Hospital consultant's room*

A massive file of DIANA'S *case history is lying on a desk. A female consultant,* DOCTOR ROPER, *is seated on her desk and swinging her legs, while flicking through the file.* DERIC, *looking a little anxious, is seated opposite her.*

DR ROPER'S VOICE She must be the most written about woman in history apart from Joan Collins . . .

DERIC Where is she?

DOCTOR ROPER *gives him a probing, disapproving stare.*

DR ROPER You are an anxious husband, aren't you, Mr Longden?

A pause. DERIC *suffers – anxiously.*

DERIC You still haven't told me!

DR ROPER Goodness me! A nurse is bringing her!

DERIC Good. Thank you. Because if she is, she'll have

to be careful dressing her. Just getting a sleeve on can break a finger . . .

DR ROPER   *(a patronising smile)* I was wrong. Not an anxious husband: an over-anxious one.

DERIC   So far, three hospitals have broken three.

DR ROPER   *(an irritated beat)* Tell me. How do you manage without sex?

DERIC   *(blankly)* Without . . .?

DOCTOR ROPER *flicks through the file, coolly.*

DR ROPER   I just wondered if it contributes to your anxiety: (a) a lot, or (b) a little . . .

DERIC   (c) not at all. We do have sex.

DR ROPER   *(puzzled)* How?

DERIC   Wearing roller skates as a rule. How about you?

DOCTOR ROPER *begins to bridle behind the smile.*

DR ROPER   Mr Longden, it's a perfectly valid question for a consultant to . . .

DERIC   I must tell Karen – a girl in my factory. She'd qualify as a consultant in two minutes.

DOCTOR ROPER *walks back round her desk and sits in her chair. She turns to the closing pages of* DIANA'S *file.*

DR ROPER   Some of the specialists suggest that your attitude to the patient might be making her worse. Your stress exacerbates hers, and her stress could well be the cause . . .

The door opens and a NURSE *wheels in* DIANA, *fully clothed for going home, and carries her overnight case.*

Scene Sixteen

DR ROPER   Thank you, nurse.

DIANA   Come on, love. Before I throw up. *(calmly, to* DOCTOR ROPER*)* He keeps me alive. And sane. And a human being. *(beat)* He's the only one that does.

A bitter pause.

DR ROPER   Mrs Longden, all our specialists agree that you ought to let the Maudsley Clinic in London do some tests . . .

DIANA   What do they say's wrong with me?

DR ROPER   *(evasively)* The report's long and very complicated.

DIANA   And says what?

An awkward pause.

DR ROPER   Hysteria.

A longer pause. DIANA *and* DERIC *smile wryly at each other.*

DIANA   It's all in the mind?

Tears of despair, anger and helplessness well up in DIANA'S *eyes. Silence, apart from the hospital sounds echoing outside the room.*

DIANA   They're wrong.

DERIC *gets up.*

DERIC   Let's go home, kid . . . crack open a teabag . . .

DIANA *(to* DOCTOR ROPER)   If the Maudsley Clinic reads that it's hysteria, I've had it before I start . . .

DOCTOR ROPER *knows it's true. Doesn't answer.*

DIANA   Haven't I?

Still no answer.

DIANA   *(yelling)* Haven't I, woman?!!

DOCTOR ROPER, *angered by guilt and defensiveness, screams back – even louder.*

DR ROPER   Please don't get hysteri . . .

She stops herself too late. DERIC *and* DIANA *smile in sad vindication. Then* DOCTOR ROPER *realises the irony and smiles, too. A pause. She is chastened.*

DR ROPER   It's professionally unethical for me to remove a colleague's conclusions from a patient's file . . .

A defeated pause. DIANA *turns to* DERIC.

DIANA   Home time?

DERIC   Home time.

He gets up, picks up her case and starts wheeling her towards the door. DOCTOR ROPER *watches, her professionalism battling with her sympathy. Her sympathy wins.*

DR ROPER   Perhaps you can do me a favour?

They turn. She avoids their eyes and hands DERIC *the file.*

DR ROPER   Could you pop it in Reception for me on your way out? *(beat)* It's . . . um . . . the last five pages.

DERIC *and* DIANA *grin.* DOCTOR ROPER *manages to avoid grinning back.* DERIC *takes the file.*

DIANA   Thanks.

DERIC *wheels her out.*

In the hospital toilet DIANA *is in her wheelchair, ripping the last five pages out of the report with her teeth. With immense, grunting effort she stuffs them behind her back. She calls out.*

DIANA Mission accomplished, love! Over and out!

In reception DERIC *drops* DIANA'S *file on the desk. The* RECEPTIONIST *and* PASSERS-BY *watch in some bemusement as* DERIC *wheels* DIANA *faster and faster towards the exit . . . finally breaking into a mad gallop.*

17 The Longdens' house

DERIC *is seated in the bathroom at an ironing-board on which is perched his typewriter. He's briskly typing a magazine article.* DIANA *is immersed in the bath, reading the pages stolen from the report which are propped up on the soap tray across the bath in front of her. The more she reads, the more despondent she gets. She makes a small, frustrated cry.* DERIC *promptly stops typing and jerks his eyes worriedly towards her.*

DERIC Pain?

DIANA Only from reading this damn thing. If I'd wanted Dante's Inferno, I could have got it from the library.

She sweeps them bitterly from the bath on to the floor.

DIANA Five whole pages . . . and all they say is 'no idea, no cure, no hope'.

They look at each other . . . and try to smile.

DIANA How's the article going?

DERIC *(lying)* Um . . . fine . . . very good . . .

Her concern now becomes concern for him. The phone rings. DERIC *calls towards the door.*

DERIC Sally?

SALLY *is cleaning the kitchen – which means she's up to her eyes in utter chaos: buckets, mops, cloths, cleaning liquids are scattered around. A bomb site. Whichever way she turns she sends something flying. She hears the phone.*

SALLY   It'll be Steve! It'll be Steve!

She knocks a bucket over on her way out, and grabs the phone in the hall.

SALLY   *(into phone – seductively)* If that's the man who worships the air I walk on, hi lover . . . If it's anybody else, you can go and get . . .

Cut to DERIC'S *office at the factory.* SHEILA *is seated at* DERIC'S *desk, a letter in her hand, speaking into the phone.*

SHEILA   *(into phone)* Oh, is that young Sally? *(beat)* Sheila at the factory. I was after your dad. And shouldn't that be 'the ground' you walk on or am I old-fashioned? *(pause)* Oh, I see. Well, it's nice to be happy. No, it's all right, you can give him a message if you will. Ask him which does he want first – the good news or the bad?

18 The factory

In contrast to our last visit, the machinists' room is now a buzzing, frenetic blur of activity. All the girls are working flat out. DERIC *is cutting material at a bench.* SHEILA *alternates between collecting* DERIC'S *pieces to give to the girls to sew, or collecting finished work from them. The radio is blasting away.*

JOAN *appears at the office door, holding an open desk diary in her hand. She signals to* DERIC *and goes back in.* DERIC *puts his shears down on the bench and follows her into the office.*

JOAN *pores over the desk diary which is lying on top of a filing cabinet.* DERIC *pops his head in.*

DERIC   You called, madam?

JOAN *(referring to diary and letters)* The VAT want to inspect your books on the twenty-seventh. Eleven a.m. Have I to pencil it in?

DERIC Yes. Can I go now? You know how big an order it is, I have to . . .

JOAN It's not how big it is, lad, it's how fast he wants it delivered.

DERIC Exactly. So if you'll excuse me.

JOAN It's not Mr Margolis's fault.

DERIC I didn't say it was.

JOAN He's only ordered it out of pity. You should've wangled it out of him months back, then we wouldn't all have our knickers in a twist.

DERIC Are you trying to make me feel better?

JOAN No.

DERIC Good. You've succeeded.

He goes – then promptly pops his head back in again.

DERIC I was wrong about the twenty-seventh. I'm out of action on the twenty-seventh. Literary luncheon.

He goes.

JOAN 'Luncheon'! Get him.

19 The Longdens' street

NICK'S *Cortina hurtles down the street – passing* SALLY, *who's trudging along weighed down with shopping. She calls and waves to him with a bulging carrier bag to attract his attention – and fails. The car slams to a stop next to the Citroën outside the house.* NICK *piles out.*

In the kitchen DERIC *is emptying the tumble dryer of dry washing and loading it with a new batch of wet. We hear* NICK *burst in at the front door. He barges into the kitchen.*

NICK   (*urgently*) Have we any black shoe polish?

DERIC *gapes at him, dumbstruck.* NICK *starts searching in drawers and cupboards.*

NICK   Where do we keep it?

DERIC   You've never polished your shoes in your life! Your mum's been begging you for nineteen years . . .

NICK   She's been begging you longer. I need it fast, Dad! Where is it?

By now DERIC *is also rummaging randomly through drawers and cupboards.*

DERIC   How would I know? What the hell's brought this on? You're not getting married today, are you?

NICK   We have fixed a day, by the way.

DERIC *immediately stops searching.*

DERIC   Hey! When?

NICK *notices an old biscuit tin that* DERIC *has dragged out of a cupboard and is still holding.*

NICK   Good lad! Well done!

DERIC   Pardon?

NICK   That's it.

DERIC   What's what?

NICK   (*grabbing the tin*) I remember it. The day I joined the Scouts. Mum polished them.

He plonks it on the work surface, yanks off the lid, pulls out a tin of black polish and a duster and starts for the door.

DERIC   When's the wedding, then?

NICK   I've a chance of flogging the car, you see. Trick of the trade – you polish the gasket on the rocker cover. Clean engine – quick sale!

SALLY *staggers in with her shopping bags.*

SALLY   Well, thanks for the lift, you great . . .

But NICK *has already squeezed past her and gone. She dumps the shopping on the work surface, grumbling.*

DERIC   They've finally picked a day, it seems.

SALLY   (*delighted*) No! When??

Just as DERIC *is replacing the lid on the tin, he catches sight of something tucked away among the other polishes. He freezes.*

SALLY   Dad! When is it?!

DERIC   Um . . . He didn't say . . .

SALLY   What?!

She drops whatever she's holding and dashes from the room and DERIC *takes from the tin the object that attracted his attention – and has turned his stomach. It's a bottle of yellow Soneral sleeping pills.*

In the bedroom the Soneral bottle is now in DIANA'S *hands, her fingers almost caressing it. She's sitting up in bed.* DERIC *stands at the window, facing the street. A solemn, pain-filled pause.*

DERIC   (*quietly – his back to her*) Have you got any more hidden?

DIANA No, love.

DERIC *(wretchedly)* You always said . . . if it comes to . . . if it came to . . . You said it won't be behind my back.

DIANA It won't, love. Wouldn't. You'd be the first to know.

He turns, comes to the bed and sits beside her. He gently prises the bottle from her fingers, puts it in his pocket, then holds her hand in his. A small, sad smile.

DERIC Weren't daft, were you? The one place we'd never look . . .

DIANA Clever these Chinese. Where was it?

DERIC In the shoe po . . .

He stops – and stares at her in shock.

DERIC You have got more hidden!!

Diana grimaces ruefully at her faux pas.

DIANA Oops! Not so bloody clever . . .

DERIC Where, Diana?! Where've you put the others she gave you?! Tell me!

She sighs, deeply, resignedly. The confession – and confrontation – she hoped to avoid is inescapable.

DIANA Deric. Love. You always, always understand how I feel – everything – so well. Except for one thing.

DERIC Diana! Where've you put them?!

DIANA It's the one thing I want to be able to do – on my own.

DERIC Well, I don't! I bloody don't!

DIANA   That's sod all to do with it!

DERIC   We haven't to give up, Diana! Ever!

DIANA   When I want to, yes, Deric. If I decide.

DERIC   That's why it's not up to you! Can't you see?! For that very reason!

DIANA   No! That's why it has to be! For the same, self-same, bloody, bloody reason!

SALLY *bursts in, emitting a fanfare.*

SALLY   March twenty-fourth! Official! Wedding bells!

DIANA *struggles to appear excited.* DERIC *turns away.*

DIANA   Hey!!

NICK *shuffles in, face and shirt smudged with black polish.*

NICK   I was going to tell them . . .!

SALLY   *(to her parents)* What's wrong?

DERIC *turns to face her.*

DERIC   *(smiling)* March twenty-fourth, eh?

NICK   *(to both parents)* What's happened?

DERIC   And when were you going to tell us? March the twenty-fifth?

SALLY *and* NICK *share a wry, defeated glance – aware that their parents' defences are not going to be dropped.*

DIANA   Which church?

SALLY/NICK   St Luke's.

DIANA   How long's the aisle?

SALLY/NICK   What?

DIANA   *(to* DERIC*)* Get me up, love! I've to start practising!

He carefully helps her out of bed. NICK *helps – though neither he nor* SALLY *knows what she's talking about.*

SALLY   Practising what?

DIANA   Watch!

Supported by DERIC *and* NICK*, she takes a very tentative half-step. It takes a massive, agonising effort. She then subsides sideways into* DERIC'S *arms.* SALLY *and* NICK *cheer and applaud.* DERIC *holds her in his arms, triumphantly.*

DERIC   That's the spirit! *(pointedly)* More the spirit!

DIANA   For me, though! That's why. My own boss.

DERIC   What?

DIANA   Because it's what I want!

DERIC *resignedly takes her point.* NICK *and* SALLY *are still bewildered by the running skirmish.*

NICK   What are you two on about?

Though excited, DIANA *is exhausted and in pain. As* NICK *and* SALLY *lay her back on the bed,* DERIC *is watching all three of them. He's never seen them so happy. Suddenly his publicly hidden depression floods over him, his smile drops and his eyes become haunted again.*

DERIC   *(to himself)* Playing 'Happy Families', are we? Eh? That what you're doing?

SALLY *throws him a glance, as though she didn't quite catch what he said.* DERIC *promptly reassumes his public smile.* SALLY *smiles back and returns her attention to* DIANA. DERIC *continues to smile . . . but his eyes stay haunted.*

20 Hotel lounge – literary lunch

A noisy, sociably over-cheerful mêlee of people having drinks and shouted, polite conversations above the babble, before going into their lunch. Introductions are made, hands shaken, jokes exchanged. Waitresses swerve through them with trays of drinks and crisps.
DERIC *stands alone, looking a little out of place, but smiling as though he isn't. He tries, and fails, to grab a drink as the tray is wafted past him. This is only the second time we've seen him wearing a tie.*

Through the throng he catches sight of an attractive, curvaceous woman in her mid-thirties. Her long, wavy hair is the colour of autumn. She's standing with a small group of women. She laughs with such open, sheer pleasure that it seems her whole body is laughing.

DERIC *can't take his eyes off her. Suddenly she turns and faces him – and smiles point blank at him. He looks away fractionally, then can't resist turning back. She's still smiling at him.*

This is AILEEN ARMITAGE. *He starts towards her, with attempted nonchalance, as though simply going that way by chance. As he hovers nearby* . . .

AILEEN *(to her friends)* Oh, I think Lycra body-stockings are even worse . . .

She turns – directly to DERIC.

AILEEN Don't you find they pull you up by the crutch?

DERIC *is gobsmacked. She seems to be waiting for a reply.*

DERIC Um . . . I don't wear body-stockings . . .

AILEEN Oh, I'm sorry. I didn't realise you were a man.

She turns back to her friends. DERIC *is stunned. The* MAITRE D' *calls from the back of the lounge.*

MAITRE D' Ladies and gentlemen, luncheon is served.

In the dining room the guests are milling round their tables, searching for their place-names. DERIC *wanders through, peering at table numbers until he spots the one he's allocated to. He smiles his fixed, fatuous smile at his fellow-diners, already seated, then sits down.*

He glances at the person next to him. It's AILEEN. *(She's smoking a cigarette.) He sits down.*

DERIC   Hello again.

AILEEN   *(her infectious smile)* Oh, hello.

DERIC   Um . . . I'm Deric Longden.

AILEEN   Lovely to meet you. I'm Aileen Armitage, I –

DERIC   *(impressed)* You're Aileen Armitage?

AILEEN   Yes. I'm a novelist.

DERIC   No, you're not. You're a fantastic novelist!

AILEEN   *(grins)* I think I'm going to like you, Mr Longden . . .

An army of waitresses, bearing bowls of soup, burst with a great clatter, out of the kitchens. One WAITRESS *is black and eager and speaks in a broad Yorkshire accent. She races towards* DERIC'S *table.*

WAITRESS   *(as she serves)* I'm sorry if it tastes cold, but it weren't all that hot when they dolloped it out. Y'ave to forgive 'em . . . it's the pressure. *(confidentially)* This chef. If he has to open more than one tin of anything he goes to pieces. *(pause)* They said it's mushroom, but don't take bets. *(to* AILEEN*)* I like your frock.

AILEEN   *(pleased)* Thank you.

WAITRESS   Which is yours?

AILEEN   Which what?

WAITRESS   Which feller?

AILEEN   *(tapping* DERIC*)* This one.

The WAITRESS *surveys* DERIC.

WAITRESS   I've seen worse. He reminds me of my dad. My dad's white. You wouldn't think so to look at me, would you?

AILEEN   *(puzzled)* Wouldn't I?

DERIC *is puzzled by this reply. The* WAITRESS *ignores it.*

WAITRESS   Bon appetite. Get plenty of bread rolls down you. It'll hide the taste.

She rushes off. AILEEN *turns to* DERIC.

AILEEN   She sounded nice. Is there an ashtray?

DERIC *slides one across the table towards her.*

DERIC   One ashtray.

AILEEN   Ta.

She promptly stubs her cigarette out in the sugar bowl.

AILEEN   Oh! Sorry about that.

DERIC   *(blankly)* Didn't you see it?

AILEEN   *(simply, matter-of-factly)* No. I can't – see anything. Well, in a good light I can see sort of blobs. Instead of faces. Yours seems quite a nice blob . . .

She smiles. DERIC *stares, shocked.*

Ten minutes later, in the dining room, the swing doors from the kitchen open, and the army of waitresses pours out again, carrying empty trays. They disperse to their different tables to collect the soup bowls. The black WAITRESS *races to* DERIC'S *table.*

WAITRESS   The latest theory is that it was leek and potato . . .

She starts collecting the bowls. As she reaches DERIC *and* AILEEN, *she notices their soup bowls are still full.*

WAITRESS   Have you finished?

DERIC/AILEEN   Yes, thanks.

WAITRESS   You haven't touched it, either of you. *(she beams)* Still, you don't when you're in love, do you?

She carries off their plates – oblivious to the effect her innocuous remark has had on them.

Outside we see that the hotel is perched on the edge of a moor. Sunlight shines through a thin moorland mist. It's about three hours later. Guests are leaving the luncheon, getting into their cars and driving off. DERIC *and* AILEEN *are among them.*

AILEEN   You're sure it's on your way home . . . the Huddersfield road?

DERIC   Absolutely certain. Mind you, I've no sense of direction.

He opens the passenger door of his Citroën.

DERIC   In you go. It's a Rolls Royce, by the way. Pink.

AILEEN *gets in.*

AILEEN   You're lying, Longden. It doesn't feel pink.

DERIC *laughs and gets into the driver's seat.*
    DERIC *switches on the engine. It coughs and splutters, but refuses to start.*

AILEEN   It doesn't feel like a Rolls Royce.

DERIC *starts to get out.*

DERIC   I'll just give it a push – show it who's boss.

AILEEN   Shall I steer?

DERIC   *(a puzzled beat)* Steer??

AILEEN   You have to treat unsighted people as though they're normal, Mr Longden. Otherwise we have this tendency to turn violent and call out of the window that we're being raped. It's up to you.

DERIC   *(laughing)* Go on, then. It's in neutral and the ignition's on.

He gets out. AILEEN *clambers into the driver's seat.*

   DERIC *jams his shoulder against the car's window-frame and starts pushing. The car rolls very slowly forward. Suddenly it begins to gather speed.* DERIC *is puzzled. He jerks a look to the rear of the car and sees three of the luncheon guests, in their best suits, helpfully pushing the car.*

DERIC   *(alarmed)* No . . . No, don't!

1ST GUEST   *(calling to* AILEEN*)* Shove it into second gear, missus! Now!

DERIC   She can't!!

The car is now speeding, freewheeling, towards the edge of a small cliff. In mounting panic, DERIC *tries to pull the car back by the window-frame. The three guests at the back see they're heading towards the railings.*

2ND GUEST   Tell her to look where she's going!

DERIC   She's blind!

The three men boggle in horror.

DERIC *(yelling to Aileen)* Pull the wheel to the left!

She does so. Just in time. The car swerves violently away from the railings. Two of the three men go flying to the ground . . . and the car is flying headlong straight towards a parked car.

DERIC *(yelling)* Now brake! Hard! Brake!

AILEEN *does so. The car screams to a sudden stop. The third man hurtles on to the boot by his own momentum.* DERIC *leans against the window, panting and trembling.* AILEEN *beams at him.*

AILEEN *(happily)* See! Told you I could steer.

21 Street in Huddersfield

AILEEN'S *flat is part of a large house in a street of dignified Victorian houses in Huddersfield. The Citroën comes driving down the street and stops outside.* DERIC *is at the wheel,* AILEEN *in the passenger seat.*

DERIC Number 31, madam, service with a smile.

AILEEN Are you smiling?

DERIC Can't you tell?

AILEEN Hang on.

She positions herself comfortably facing him and starts to trace the features of his face with gently stroking fingertips.

AILEEN Funny nose.

DERIC Not very good at this, are you?

AILEEN And ears.

DERIC Not very good at all.

AILEEN Sexy mouth.

DERIC You're improving.

AILEEN Deep laugh lines . . . that's what matters.

DERIC D'you mean wrinkles?

AILEEN *laughs. A pause.*

AILEEN Well, thanks for the lift.

DERIC My pleasure. It worked wonders for my laugh lines.

AILEEN And you've got my phone number in case you do fancy writing something together?

DERIC Yep. *(beat)* And you've memorised mine?

AILEEN Yes.

DERIC Sure?

AILEEN Put it this way . . . If you get a call asking you to come and mend a tumble dryer, you'll know I've got it wrong.

He laughs. Another pause.

AILEEN Well . . . it was smashing to meet you, Mr Longden.

DERIC You, too, Mrs Armitage.

Pause.

AILEEN So . . . I'll love you and leave you.

DERIC *(quietly)* Will you?

*The moment – and its meaning – seems to hang in the air. Then,
AILEEN smiles and starts to go.*

DERIC Hang on.

She stops. He leans towards her and starts tracing his fingertips over her face.

AILEEN (*laughs*) You don't need to do that!

DERIC (*solemnly*) Oh, yes, I do.

Her laugh subsides into an equally solemn silence. She gets out of the car.

DERIC Can you manage?

AILEEN I have till now.

DERIC (*beat*) I meant to get to the flat.

AILEEN (*smiles*) Yes, I know you did. See you.

He watches her as she walks to the flat, takes a key from her handbag, opens the door and goes in. The door closes behind her.
  DERIC *sits, staring ahead, making no move to drive off. He seems confused, disturbed, even frightened.*

22 Interior of Aileen's flat – a little later

In the kitchen AILEEN *is making a mug of tea . . . her fingers tentatively locating the teabag, then circling the rim of the mug. She drops the teabag in, then puts the tip of her index finger into the mug to test the level of the boiling water she's pouring in from the kettle. As ever, she scalds her finger.*

AILEEN Ow!!

She holds the milk bottle's neck against the rim of the mug to pour in the milk. Her fingers trace their way to the sugar and spoon. She tentatively negotiates a spoonful of sugar into the mug, stirs and takes out the teabag. She takes the mug and pushes hard with her shoulder against the living-room door which rubs against the carpet.

AILEEN Damn door!

AILEEN *feels her way to her chair, feels for a small table to put her mug on and sits down. She feels for the mug again, picks it up and sips her tea, staring unseeing into space.*

AILEEN   Don't even think about it . . .

23 Department store, Matlock

January sales. DERIC *is wheeling* DIANA *through the entrance of the store. It is packed with shoppers.*

DERIC   And she said I should have a go at writing about you . . . all about the illness and so forth . . . A TV series . . . Not a medical series, exactly, with doctors and nurses having a quick cuddle behind the X-ray machine . . . More, you know, exploring all the sort of human story and –

DIANA   Deric. You're burbling a bit.

They arrive at a lift and DERIC *wheels* DIANA *inside. The door clangs shut. The lift is packed. No one can move.*

DERIC   Or . . . she said she'd even consider writing it with me. *(to woman next to lift buttons)* Four please. *(to Diana)* I'd just tell her all about you and –

DIANA   I think you have already.

DERIC   Only the dirty bits.

DIANA   I like her novels.

DERIC   I told her.

DIANA   Fancy her being blind . . .

DERIC   I know.

DIANA   I expect she must be if she took a shine to you,

mind you. *(laughs)* By hell, Deric, you can't 'alf pick 'em, can't you? Still, it'd give me a weekend off.

He laughs. The lift stops and everyone bundles out.

DERIC   Me, burbling a bit!

The January sales are in full swing and the store is packed. DERIC *weaves the wheelchair between shoppers who make no attempt to get out of the way and propels* DIANA *to the millinery department. There are scores of hats on display. An* ASSISTANT *starts to help* DIANA *to choose one.* DERIC *hovers for a moment, then takes out a shopping list and wanders off towards other departments.*

Half an hour or so later. DERIC, *with a couple of weighty shopping bags, is at the top of a down-escalator. He spots his* MOTHER *advancing towards him on the up-escalator, that runs alongside. She has a basket of shopping.*

DERIC   Morning, Mrs Longden.

She looks as though she may possibly have seen him somewhere before, but can't quite place the face. A moment or so later, as they pass, it dawns on her who he is.

MOTHER   Oh, hello, love! I knew it was somebody.

They pass each other. MOTHER *takes a carton of yoghurt from her basket.*

MOTHER   Look at this! 'Sell by the 11th' it says.

DERIC   Today's only the ninth.

MOTHER   I know. I thought I should go and tell them.

MOTHER *disappears into the crowd at the top of the escalator.*

DERIC *arrives with his shopping bags at the counter in the millinery department, but there's no sign of* DIANA. *For a moment he panics, wheeling round trying to spot her among the shoppers. An* ELDERLY MAN *is passing.*

ELDERLY MAN   Is something wrong, lad?

DERIC   I've lost my wife.

ELDERLY MAN   I lost mine in 1968. Never had a day's illness in her life. Took me nearly two weeks to get over it.

He goes on his way.

DIANA'S VOICE   Well? What's the verdict?

DERIC *turns round – to see the* ASSISTANT *wheeling* DIANA *towards him. She's wearing a sensational red hat, with feathers and veil. She's bursting with pleasure.*

DERIC   *(beams)* Made for you! Where were you?

DIANA   Looking for matching gloves. For the minute, I completely forgot about these . . .

'These' are the ungloveable Fred's hands. His heart goes out to her. But she's still euphoric.

DIANA   So what? We bought a hat!!

DERIC *is wheeling* DIANA *through the crowds outside. She holds her hat above her head as though it were the F A Cup.*

DIANA   *(chanting)* We-bought-a-hat! We-bought-a-hat! Ee-i-adio! We-bought-a-hat!

Other pedestrians apprehensively give them a wide berth.

DERIC   *(to the pedestrians)* Apparently we bought a hat.

24 *Interior of the Citroën, traffic jam*

DERIC *and* DIANA *are on their way home, but stuck solid in a traffic jam.* DIANA'S *wearing her red hat, the price tag still dangling from it, happily admiring herself in the sun visor mirror.*

DIANA   I look beautiful.

DERIC   You do. Very beautiful.

DIANA   I know. I just told you. *(pause)* So, did you fancy her then? Don't say, 'who'?

DERIC   *(meaningful pause)* 'Course I did.

He looks at her and smiles.

DIANA   Just checking. Nice to know you haven't lost all your faculties. D'you know what I'd like to do now? Go dancing.

She falls immediately asleep, the price tag bobbing in front of her nose. DERIC *glances at her – again deeply moved.*

The traffic begins to nudge forward, but DERIC'S *lane soon stops. The next lane carries on moving for a little longer, then stops. Beside the Citroën is a van with a Huddersfield address painted on its side.*

DERIC *glances out of his window and sees the van. His stomach tightens with guilt. He glances at* DIANA, *but for a moment sees* AILEEN *sitting there. A car horn blasts behind him – the jam has cleared. He slams his foot down on the accelerator – too hard, and blasts his car horn angrily back, even though he knows he's in the wrong.* DIANA *stirs fitfully.*

25 *The factory*

All the girls – except KAREN *– are idle again, reading paperbacks, chatting, attending to their make-up. In contrast,* KAREN *is working frantically, sewing a garment (her cotton keeps breaking) under* JOAN'S *tense – and irritating – supervision.*

DERIC'S VOICE   For Christ's sake! Still one to come! What're you playing at in there! How long's it take to run a frigging seam up?!!

SCENE TWENTY-FIVE

In the office DERIC *and* SHEILA *are packing the finished garments, in stacks of a dozen or so, in cardboard boxes.* DERIC *is working maniacally;* SHEILA, *slowing and methodically.*

SHEILA About as long as it'd take you to wash your mouth out with salt and water.

DERIC *(tensely)* Sheila. You all want your . . .

SHEILA Not like you, this. It's a Deric Longden I don't know. Haven't had the dubious privilege of meeting before. . .

DERIC *(even more tensely)* You all want your wages tomorrow, I've to get these to Manchester today. This afternoon! Henry's going spare!

In his haste, he accidentally knocks a pile of the folded garments to the floor.

DERIC Jesus!

He starts scrabbling them back up again, SHEILA *shoots him an old-fashioned look and re-folds them. The sound of* KAREN'S *machine next door suddenly stops. He yells towards the door.*

DERIC Well, come on, then!!

JOAN *walks in, carrying* KAREN'S *finished garment.*

JOAN A stitch in time. *(grins)* D'you get it?

SHEILA *laughs,* DERIC *doesn't. He grabs it for packing with the others. She and* JOAN *share an old-fashioned look and load his arms up with the now packed boxes. He heads for the door.*

DERIC *comes from the office and goes straight to the exit door, and out.*

KAREN You're welcome. Don't mention it. Our pleasure.

26 The Longdens' house

In the living room DIANA *is propped up on the settee, her legs stretched out in front of her, trying to hand-sew a bridesmaid's dress. This is an even more pitiably tortuous process than painting her fingernails. She uses her teeth and both hands. The effort, pain and frustration of completing one stitch exhausts her. She begins to weep quietly.*

She hears the sound of an approaching car, which then stops outside. Footsteps. Then the front door opening. She struggles to bite back her sobs.

DERIC'S VOICE   Only whatsisname!

We hear the front door close again. With a huge effort, DIANA *manages to wipe her tears with the bridesmaid's dress and assume a cheerful smile just as* DERIC *walks in. He, too, is playing the same game. Outwardly, calm and at ease; inwardly, even more nerve-racked and tense than he was in the factory.*

DIANA   I thought it was Manchester-here-you-come?

DERIC   It is.

He sits beside her and kisses her.

DIANA   What're you doing here, then?

DERIC   This. *(kisses her again)* D'you want a cup of tea or anything before I go? *(calls towards the kitchen)* Sally?

DIANA   She's out.

DERIC *is immediately disconcerted.*

DIANA   Joanne wanted her to go to town with her . . . for her bottom drawer.

DERIC   Just today?! The wedding's weeks off!! She promised she'd —

DIANA   She'll be back in an hour or two. Soon as she's bought every pair of coloured tights in town. Go on. I'm fine.

He stays put, concerned at leaving her on her own. He indicates her sewing.

DERIC   How's it going?

DIANA   I can't do it, love. The one thing I was ever any good at . . . Not to worry. Naked bridesmaids are all the rage in California.

A forlorn pause. DERIC *knows that this decision is as painful to her as her physical pain.*

DERIC   *(abruptly)* Come on. On your feet.

DIANA   Sewing standing up's no easier . . .

He gently gets her to her feet and holds her upright.

DERIC   From here to the telly. If it's racing from Kempton Park you get to kick it in.

DIANA   Deric. Manchester. Go.

DERIC   A few minutes'll make no odds.

Unseen by DIANA, *he nevertheless glances at his watch, as he holds her and she slowly makes her first step.*

DERIC   Fantastic! One small step for Mrs Longden, a giant V-sign for mankind!

DIANA   *(excited – scared)* It wasn't on my own, though . . .

She nevertheless takes another step. It exhausts her.

DERIC   Enough! All in good time. You've to learn to walk before you can walk.

DIANA *(suddenly solemn)* Deric . . . Give it a rest. Me a rest.

DERIC *(puzzled)* The walking? *(beat)* It was me that said 'Enough' . . . !

DIANA Not the walking.

DERIC What, then?

DIANA It's for me to say 'Enough'. Or not. As the case may be. Or to hell with it. Or . . . or . . . whatever I . . . Something has to be mine, Deric. My doing. My say-so.

A perturbed, frustrated silence. Frustrated for both of them.

DIANA I don't mean the walking, love. I don't really know what I mean . . . *(beat)* Go on, skedaddle, she'll be home soon.

DERIC I'll pop you in bed, then. Get your strength back.

DIANA Deric! Mr Margolis. Shoo.

DERIC Plenty of time. Come on.

He picks her up to carry her upstairs.

DIANA You'll get stuck in the rush hour!

DERIC No problem.

Once again he glances surreptitiously at his watch.

27 *Interior of the travelling Citroën – Dusk*

The speedometer is registering 90 mph – and rising. DERIC *is at the wheel. His face is frozen in a mask of silently screaming tension. He hears laughter. His eyes flick to the driving mirror. He sees himself sitting in the back seat, laughing. He turns round, but his* ALTER EGO *has gone.*

DERIC'S VOICE Sell the factory, that's it . . . In hot water. . . Put the immersion heater on. . . Give Diana a hot bath every hour. . . In the night. . . Keep awake. . . Tumble dryer on. . . In hot water. . . In the red. . . Red hat for the wedding. . . Oh. Love. . . Love's blind. . . Can't see. . . See Aileen – no! Don't see Aileen.

We hear the laughter once more. DERIC *spins round, sees his* ALTER EGO *laughing even harder. He turns on the radio to drown out the laughter. But the sight of his* ALTER EGO *laughing soundlessly is even more frightening. He switches the radio off again.*

DERIC'S ALTER EGO *(reflection in mirror)* You can't drive away from me, pal. However fast you go. I'm the one you can't run away from.

He glances beside him – and sees DIANA, *in her red hat, in the passenger seat. He faces front . . . then looks towards the passenger seat again. Now it's* AILEEN *who's sitting there. He suddenly begins to cry. Quietly, at first, keening. Then in shuddering, racking sobs. He starts to cry out.*

  The Citroën scorches along, then swerves suddenly across the road. It skids round once then bounces drunkenly to a stop, its nose submerged in a water-filled ditch. DERIC *heaves the door open. He half-climbs, half-falls out of the car, staggers up out of the stagnant water and collapses on the muddy verge.*

It is night. DERIC *is sitting in the mud, leaning against the underside of the car that sticks up out of the ditch. He is staring into the darkness. A trickle of blood is running down his face.* DERIC *bangs the car's bodywork.*

DERIC   Are you listening in there? *(pause)* What's up? Couldn't stand the pace? *(pause)* See? *(pause)* Run fast enough, you can run away... Even if it is in a bloody circle. Anyway, I'm okay now, so you can sod off... I hate backseat drivers.

DERIC'S *face is suddenly lit up with blinding white light. He raises his hand to shield his eyes. The white light grows bigger and bigger. The light is now joined by a deafening roar, as out of the blackness emerges a vast yellow earthmover. The* DRIVER *climbs down from the cab and comes over to* DERIC. *He kneels down.*

DRIVER   You all right, lad?

DERIC *nods.*

DRIVER   You look like you could do with a doctor.

DERIC *laughs; the man doesn't understand.*

DERIC   *(getting up)* Sorry. Private joke.

28 Mother's house

A crisp, sunny winter's day. DIANA *is in her wheelchair, in the back doorway of the little terraced house. She is struggling once again to hand-sew a dress (different material; this is to be her own for the wedding). She also seems to be struggling with her thoughts.*

DERIC'S MOTHER *is propping up an ironing-board, at its lowest setting, on an overgrown flowerbed; its legs in the soil, straddling above the crocuses and daffodils. Beside it there's a trowel, a weeding fork and a bucket. She then lies full length, face down, on the ironing-board and starts weeding the soil on one side of it.*

As she weeds, the ironing-board's legs begin to sink slowly into the soft soil . . . descending until it's completely flat on the ground – and squashing dead all the flowers under it.

DIANA *watches all this, deadpan.* MOTHER *then rolls herself off the ironing-board and on to the grass.*

DIANA It's an interesting time to be weeding, Mum. The middle of winter.

MOTHER *(whispered)* I like to catch 'em off-guard.

DIANA You've got a thing about ironing-boards, you and your son.

MOTHER Very good for weeding, isn't it?

DIANA It kills the flowers quicker than the weeds do.

MOTHER That's the only drawback.

DIANA *(trying to sew)* Damn!

MOTHER You want me to pull your needle through again, love?

DIANA Sod that. I reckon the bridegroom's mother can go naked, an' all.

MOTHER Would you like a cup of coffee?

DIANA I'd love one.

MOTHER Are you sure? I'm having one.

DIANA All right, I will then. . . If you're having one.

MOTHER Would you prefer tea?

DIANA I wondered could I just make a phone call?

MOTHER If it's not engaged.

DIANA It can't be engaged if you're not using it, love.

MOTHER It can if it's in your bedroom. The electricity has to go uphill.

DIANA Uh-huh.

In the kitchen MOTHER *is standing by the phone;* DIANA *is in her wheelchair beside her.*

MOTHER   Who d'you want, love?

DIANA   A Miss Aileen Armitage.

MOTHER   *(beat)* I think this phone just dials numbers. It's only rented.

DIANA   *(smiles)* It's 0484 –789 – 63.

MOTHER   *(dialling)* 0484 . . .

DIANA   I think you have to pick the phone up first . . . with it being Huddersfield.

MOTHER   Oh, right. *(picks up phone)* I've forgot the numbers. I hope she appreciates all the trouble we're going to. Who is she, anyway?

29 Telephone conversation: intercut between Aileen's flat and Mother's kitchen

AILEEN *is writing at her desk. She writes in huge letters on an A4 writing pad, feeling the edge of the pad as she does so to avoid writing beyond the page and on to the desk. The phone rings loudly and abruptly. She feels across the desk for it and takes it.*

AILEEN   *(into phone)* Hello? . . . Speaking.

Mother's kitchen

MOTHER *is holding the phone for* DIANA.

DIANA   *(into phone)* It's Diana Longden here. *(beat)* Deric's wife.

Aileen's living room

AILEEN *stiffens. A beat.*

AILEEN   *(into phone)* Oh, hello, Mrs Longden.

Mother's kitchen

DIANA *takes a deep breath.*

DIANA   *(into phone)* I was wondering if we could have a little chat, Mrs Armitage.

Aileen's living room

AILEEN *cannot, on the spur of the moment, articulate a reply. She prepares herself tensely for whatever it is* DIANA *has to say . . .*

30 Optician's eye-testing room

DERIC'S MOTHER *is in the chair, facing the red and green flashing lights and the illuminated test card, while the optician slots various lenses in the contraption perched on her nose. She holds her elastoplasted glasses in her hands.*

OPTICIAN   Beyond me, this, madam. Whoever dispenses these for you's an idiot. They're entirely the wrong prescription.

MOTHER   It was you.

OPTICIAN   Pardon?

MOTHER   You're the only chiropodist I've ever been to.

OPTICIAN   'Chiropo . . .'??

MOTHER   Well it might've been your dad. Twenty-two years ago. For my husband. I've worn them nine years – since he popped his clogs.

OPTICIAN   *(beat)* You've been wearing someone else's glasses for nine years?

MOTHER Not every day. I sometimes lend them to Nellie Elliott because she won't set foot in a chiropodist's.

In the waiting room there are display cases of spectacle frames, a desk with a RECEPTIONIST *behind it, and* SALLY, *sitting waiting, reading an optician's trade magazine. After a moment, the door of the eye-testing room opens and the* OPTICIAN *comes out, still a little shell-shocked.* MOTHER *trundles out behind him.*

SALLY Okay, Gran?

MOTHER We've decided I'll just borrow Minnie Bonsall's contact lenses.

SALLY *jerks a surprised look at the* OPTICIAN.

OPTICIAN *She* decided.

MOTHER *(to Sally)* Right. Where now, chuck?

SALLY Afternoon tea with my mum. Special occasion.

MOTHER What kind of special?

SALLY That she didn't say. Come on.

MOTHER It's not my birthday, is it?

They leave. As the door closes behind them:

OPTICIAN *(to Receptionist)* It's certainly not mine.

31 Café

A WAITRESS *stands, checking the order, at a table around which are seated* DIANA, MOTHER, SALLY *and* AILEEN. AILEEN *is seated slightly apart from the others.*

WAITRESS So that's two Welsh rarebits.

MOTHER Ta.

AILEEN   Yes.

SALLY *and* MOTHER *give* AILEEN *an encouraging smile.*

WAITRESS   One chocolate éclair.

SALLY   Thanks.

WAITRESS   And . . .

She can't bring herself to look at DIANA.

WAITRESS   Would she like salad with her cheese?

SALLY *and* DIANA *share a wry glance at the customary assumption that the handicapped can't speak.*

SALLY   Please.

WAITRESS   Right.

She goes.

DIANA   *(wryly)* Bring her back. She forgot to ask you about my periods . . . *(pause)* Well, ladies. Thank you all for coming.

She looks at each of them in turn . . . her face growing a little serious.

DIANA   Now that you've both met Aileen, I expect you're wondering what this is all about. I expect Aileen is as well. So . . . I expect I'd better tell you.

Wide shot of café as DIANA *begins quietly, carefully, seriously to elaborate . . .*

32 Railway station platform

DERIC *is wheeling* DIANA *towards the waiting London train. He carries a small suitcase.*

DERIC It's barmy, love! Honest to God, it's absolutely barmy!

DIANA I'll be all right, Deric! I've got to do something on my own, sometime! All I have to do is sit here. The train does the rest.

DERIC At least let me come to King's Cross with you and get you to the Maudsley, then I'll catch the next back.

In the train compartment DERIC *is manoeuvring* DIANA *through the door into the carriage. Two or three other* PASSENGERS *studiously stare at their magazines or newspapers in order to avoid – except surreptitiously – their handicapped fellow-traveller.*

DIANA I thought we were broke?

DERIC I'll sell my body in Soho.

DIANA I wish you'd sell mine while you're at it.

The other PASSENGERS *overhear the whispered conversation . . . and look more and more uncomfortable.*

DERIC I'm not laughing, love.

DIANA Go on, before the train goes.

A pause DIANA'S *bravado is ebbing; her fear growing.*

DERIC Are you sure?

DIANA Yes. *(pause. She's on the verge of tears)* No. Come with me, love.

DERIC You won't be angry . . . that you needed me?

DIANA *(beat)* I do need you, love.

The train starts to move off. DERIC *puts the suitcase on the rack and sits beside her, his arm round her.*

DIANA *(one last stab at being brave)* I can always come back on my own. Cured. Overnight.

DERIC It's a deal.

33 Maudsley Hospital ward – Night

DERIC *is seated by the side of an empty bed, reading a magazine. A pause. Then suddenly there's the approaching sound of a commotion outside the swing doors.* DERIC *stands up apprehensively and looks towards them. They burst open and an* ORDERLY *wheels in a trolley. A* DOCTOR *and a* NURSE *run beside it.*

On it is DIANA . . . *writhing and twisting, kicking out with a foot now encased in a plaster and metal cage, her wrists crossed over her face covering her eyes, banging her head again and again against the side of the trolley.*

They race her to the bed. The NURSE *clamps* DIANA'S *head and swings her on her side.* DIANA *heaves her body up and down, arching her back. The* DOCTOR *shouts orders urgently.*

DERIC *is bundled out of the way as the medical staff finally shovel* DIANA *into her bed. The* NURSE *massages her head through a wet towel with her fingertips.*

Slowly, DIANA *quietens down.* DERIC *stares down at her, terrified.*

DERIC What happened?

DOCTOR God knows . . . she went into a convulsion. We had to abort the milogram we were giving her. New one on me. Perhaps there was pressure on the brain . . . Who knows?

He takes DIANA'S *hand and holds it gently in his and strokes it. We suddenly hear a loud crack.*

DOCTOR What was that?

DIANA *opens her eyes and speaks calmly.*

DIANA   My finger. You've just broken it.

The DOCTOR *looks, appalled, at the fingers he was so gently stroking.* DIANA *smiles wanly.*

DIANA   Sorry to sound so hysterical.

She smiles, resignedly, at DERIC, *who's now at her side.*

DIANA   Hello, love. Day one.

DERIC   Hello, sweetheart.

DIANA   Go and have a smoke.

DERIC   I don't want one.

DIANA   You're not missing a thing.

He kisses her. She flutters her eyelashes, mock coyly.

DIANA   Oh, I don't know, though . . . Go and have a beer, then.

DERIC   I don't want a beer either.

DIANA   And chat up one of the nurses.

DERIC   Oh, all right, then.

DIANA   Only one, though. You've a train to catch.

The DOCTOR *and the* NURSE *exchange worried, baffled glances.*

34 Train carriage, Matlock Railway station – Night

An Intercity train pulls into the platform. DERIC *is asleep in the corner of the compartment. An* OLD MAN *shakes* DERIC *awake.*

OLD MAN   You're here, lad.

DERIC *just manages to grab his scattered belongings and get off, before the train heads off into the night.*

35 Deric's Citroën – Night

As DERIC *drives, his mind is working overtime. He catches sight of something.* DERIC'S *car passes camera, does a sudden U-turn and heading back towards us, turns off on another road. We crane up to find a roadsign that reads: 'Huddersfield'.*

Next, in AILEEN'S *street in Huddersfield, the Citroën drives slowly up and stops.* DERIC *switches off the engine, and sits for a moment . . . very still, empty, wooden. He looks up at* AILEEN'S *window, then turns away to face front again. Then abruptly switches on the engine and drives off.*

36 The Longdens' house

In the kitchen SALLY *is ransacking shelves and cupboards, the fridge, cartons . . . grimly searching and leaving behind her a wake of chaos. She suddenly screams towards the door.*

SALLY   I hate it! I hate it, Dad! Dad, I hate it!

In the living-room NICK *is also searching . . . behind cushions, behind the TV set, in the sideboard drawers. He calls to the ceiling.*

NICK   *(a calm cover-up)* Apparently Sally isn't too keen on this, Dad.

In the bedroom DERIC *is searching everywhere – under the bed, the wardrobes, the cupboards, dressing table.*

DERIC   *(yelling down)* Just do it! All right?

SALLY, *in tears, hurls all the packets and cartons which she's put on the work surface during her search across the room. She runs out of the door.*

SALLY *runs from the kitchen and up the stairs.* NICK *comes out of the living room and follows her upstairs.*

In the bedroom DERIC *is still searching – grimly, purposefully, hastily, forcing back tears of his own.* SALLY *runs in and starts hurling across the room whatever objects* DERIC *has removed during his search.* DERIC *takes her in his arms and sits beside her on the bed, holding her.* NICK *comes in and sits on the floor in front of them, hugging his knees.*

DERIC   (*gently to Sally*) The only chance we've got is when she's in hospital. We know there was more than one lot stashed away. We have to get them before she gets the chance to, love.

SALLY   (*quietening*) It's horrible, Dad. I can't bear it.

DERIC *gets up and starts for the door.*

DERIC   I'll go and do the attic.

SALLY   Why now?! This minute! Why do we have to look for them just now?

DERIC *stops at the door. He sags.*

SALLY   (*to Nick*) If we do find them, he may swallow half of them.

NICK *jerks a scared look at her. He hadn't thought of that.*

SALLY   Or even give them to her, if she asks him to.

NICK   (*scornfully*) He worships her, you nutter!

SALLY   That's why! (*to Deric*) Would you? Is that why you want them?

DERIC   (*flatly*) To chuck them away. I'd just chuck them away.

NICK   Then she's got no way out . . . if . . . you know . . . if it ever comes to . . .

SALLY   Right.

NICK   (*shakes his head – miserably*) No, Sally. It's wrong.

37 Aileen's flat

DERIC *and* AILEEN *are seated beside each other on the settee hands gently inter-clasped.* DERIC *strokes* AILEEN'S *finger.*

DERIC   Do this to Diana's – and it breaks it. *(pause)* And your heart at the same time. *(struggling to find the words he wants)* The thing about Diana – the main thing – from the day I met her . . . however sick she is . . . she's more, more alive than anyone I've ever known. She makes me more alive. *(smiles)* Except you. You're the same. *(his smile falters)* I'm sorry to say.

A charged moment. AILEEN *breaks it.*

AILEEN   Sounds like a judicious time to make a cup of tea . . .

DERIC *promptly gets to his feet to go and make it – the role he's been playing for years.*

DERIC   Do you take sugar?

AILEEN   Don't you dare. It's my job.

She gets up. They're standing face to face. DERIC'S *troubled by their physical closeness.*

DERIC   Aileen . . .

He puts out his hand to touch her, then stops short. She senses his feelings; and laughs, again to break the moment.

AILEEN   Am I to assume a cup of tea isn't what you want at all?

DERIC   *(in turmoil)* I want . . . all I want is for her to be well and happy. And me, too . . . With her . . . What I don't want is to want you . . . I can cope, sort of, with most things . . . I can't cope with hating my bloody self.

They're both at a loss as to how to handle their conflicting emotions.

AILEEN   Tell you what. How about if I slip into something loose and . . . ?

Now it's DERIC'S *turn to divert the danger.*

DERIC   Tell me about your ex-husband . . .

AILEEN   *(laughs)* No, thanks, I'll slip into something loose and we'll —

DERIC   I promise I won't talk any more about Diana . . .

AILEEN   Let me finish! I slip into something loose – like my C & A raincoat – and we go out for a walk and you tell me everything about Diana. How's that?

He laughs – genuinely relieved.

AILEEN   Come on.

They go out of the room.
   AILEEN *gets her raincoat from the hall stand.* DERIC *holds it open for her to put on.*

DERIC   Thanks.

AILEEN   What for?

DERIC   I think they call it defusing the situation.

AILEEN   *(laughs)* My pleasure . . . Well, not pleasure exactly . . . No pleasure at all . . .

He wraps her coat around her – and his arms. He holds her and kisses her, gently at first, then with urgent, growing passion. She responds just as passionately.

38 Maudsley Hospital entrance

Several patients in wheelchairs are being wheeled out of the hospital by spouses (or parents or children). Among them is DERIC *wheeling* DIANA. *She has a small suitcase on her lap.* DIANA *looks up and down the depressing grey street.*

DIANA   Funny in'it, who'd have thought somewhere so horrible, could look so beautiful?

39 Railway terminus, London

DERIC *and* DIANA *are seated on a bench, waiting for their train. They're eating ice cream, the wheelchair parked alongside. They sit watching an* ELDERLY MAN *attending to his wheelchair-bound* WIFE. *He's kneeling beside her chair so that their faces are level . . . and they seem like young lovers.*

They laugh into each other's eyes, whisper to each other, touch each other and kiss. During this:

DIANA   The hospital's given up on me.

DERIC   I know.

DIANA   Not before I gave up on them.

DERIC   No.

DIANA   They said I could try for the world record and go to one last one. The Hospital for Nervous Diseases.

DERIC   And what did you say?

DIANA   'Oh.'

She watches the ELDERLY COUPLE, *solemnly, as they kiss.*

DIANA   That's us, Deric, in twenty years' time.

DERIC *(a beat)* Suits me, love.

40 The Longdens' bedroom

Open on DIANA'S *feet – one in a high-heeled shoe, the other in its plaster and metal cage – very slowly and tentatively walking towards* CAMERA.

DIANA's voice One shoe might be all the rage one day, like one earring . . .

We see DERIC *beside her, his hands at the ready to catch her, though not actually supporting her. She's counting each step as she goes.*

DIANA . . . three . . . four . . . five.

She stops, exhausted – though thrilled and flushed.

DIANA A week's convalescence and I might do six.

DERIC D'you want to lie down for a bit?

DIANA No. I want a Saturday afternoon treat for being good.

DERIC *(grins)* In that case I'll lie down with you.

DIANA *(laughs)* Tell you what. A run-out in the car.

DERIC McDonalds? My mother's? Blackpool illuminations?

DIANA Aileen's.

A searing bombshell of guilt, shock and apprehension explodes in the pit of DERIC'S *stomach. A beat.*

DERIC Aileen Whatshername?

DIANA Armitage. If she wants to do a play about me, she should meet me. Ring her and ask.

DERIC   You don't want to go traipsing out to . . .

DIANA   Yes, I do. Anyway, a girl likes to size up the opposition.

She waits for him to laugh. He doesn't.

DIANA   Well, laugh!

He does so – but not with his eyes.

41 Stairs to Aileen's flat

DERIC *is standing at the foot of the stairs, holding the folded wheelchair.* AILEEN *is standing at her door at the top of the stairs, peering unseeingly down.* DIANA *is part-way up the stairs, painstakingly mounting them one step at a time, on her backside, backwards.*

AILEEN   Coming upstairs on her what?

DERIC   On her own volition.

DIANA   That isn't what I said.

AILEEN   No, I thought it wasn't.

DIANA *reaches the top, with* DERIC *following up as a safety net. He helps her to her feet. She and* AILEEN *are now face to face.*

DERIC   Diana, this is Aileen. Aileen – Diana.

The two women face each other.

Ten minutes or so later. In the kitchen DERIC *is making three mugs of tea, stiff with tension, as though listening with his whole body to the sound of laughter from both* DIANA *and* AILEEN *in the living room. More than anything else, he's bewildered: they sound like two old friends. He cocks an ear . . . catching puzzling sentences from the mumble of conversation . . .*

AILEEN'S VOICE   . . . but didn't you tell me Steve was a croupier, as well?

DERIC   *(to himself)* 'Tell' her? When?

AILEEN'S VOICE   . . . Well, good for Sally! He gets better and better . . .

DERIC   *(to himself)* How does she know about Sally?

AILEEN'S VOICE   Is he still strong on the wine bar idea?

DERIC   *(to himself)* How does she know about that?

AILEEN'S VOICE   Leicester? . . . I thought you told me Nottingham?

DERIC   *(to himself)* What? 'Told' her, again. When did she tell her?

He gathers the mugs and has to push hard at the living-room door – which is still dragging on the carpet. DIANA *and* AILEEN *are seated, facing each other,* AILEEN *turns her head at the sound of the door.*

DERIC   Your door wants a bit shaving off the bottom.

DIANA   Don't we all.

AILEEN   Have you got cups in your hand?

DERIC   Only just.

She gets up to help open the door.

DIANA   Deric'll fix it for you while we go for our walk. He's a dab hand.

DERIC *distributes the mugs.*

DERIC   *(shaking his head)* You need tools for a job like that.

DIANA   Aileen's got tools. The only thing her husband didn't take with him.

DERIC *stares at her, then at* AILEEN, *then back at* DIANA.

DERIC How do you know?

The two women smile, enjoying their conspiracy.

Intercut between DERIC'S *point of view and his reactions to it. He's at the window watching* AILEEN *wheel* DIANA *to the kerb and wait for a break in the traffic.*

DIANA Okay . . . now! Down a step!

AILEEN Right!

She thumps the wheels down off the pavement and into the road. They're aiming straight for a car.

DIANA Hard right!

AILEEN Right.

They run a gauntlet of hooting, swerving, braking cars. During this:

DIANA D'you think you'll ever re-marry?

AILEEN Assuming I ever get across here in one piece? No, no, I don't.

DIANA No, don't suppose I will, either. *(beat)* Rotten, isn't it?

A van bears down on them.

DIANA Back up!!

AILEEN Right!

DIANA Now left.

AILEEN Right!

DERIC *watches all this dance with death, a screwdriver and jackplane in his hand, truly petrified for both of them.*

DERIC   Jesus . . . !

Half an hour later. AILEEN, *returns from the walk though still in her coat, gives the door a trial push.* DERIC *is pulling on the other side. It's still sticking.* DIANA'S *folded-up wheelchair is propped against a wall.*

DERIC   *(looking at the bottom of the door)* I don't understand it. I've cut nearly half an inch off . . .

AILEEN *pushes it again. It still sticks.*

AILEEN   Um . . . you haven't taken it off the top by any chance . . . ?

DERIC   Oh hell . . . she's right.

AILEEN   Brilliant. You warned me, didn't you Diana? *(she turns)* Diana?

DERIC *looks into the living room.* DIANA *is slumped on the settee, at an awkward angle; her eyes closed.* DERIC *races over to her.* AILEEN *follows.* DERIC *pulls* DIANA *upright from behind and massages her neck.*

DERIC   *(quiet urgency)* Come on, love! Wakey, wakey! You can't have blackouts in Yorkshire. They charge you.

AILEEN *is listening. Her eyes start to fill with tears.*

42 The Longdens' street

A car hurtles down the street. It screams to a halt outside the Longdens' front door. Inside is NICK'S BEST MAN, *wearing tails, a cravat, and a carnation in his buttonhole. He sits at the wheel, honking out the rhythm of 'I'm Getting Married in the Morning' on the car horn. Startled* NEIGHBOURS *peep through their windows at him.*

In the bathroom, wearing striped trousers and top hat, but bare-

chested, DERIC *is shaving at the mirror, while* SALLY, *in bra and panties and a towel round her head, is also trying to get ready. All they're really doing is getting in each other's way. Horrified, they hear the car horn's tune in the street.*

SALLY   Is that the time??

DERIC   Where's Nick?

SALLY   Still in bed.

DERIC   Not any more, he isn't!

He races out of the room. SALLY *grabs her opportunity to use the sink, undisturbed.*

In the bedroom NICK *is propped up in bed, eating a boiled egg and soldiers, still in his pyjamas, and nodding to the music he can hear through his Walkman headphones.* DERIC *bursts in. He yanks off* NICK'S *headphones and rams his top hat on his head.*

DERIC   Bloody church!!

He races out again.

In the kitchen a few minutes later DERIC'S MOTHER, *in her wedding finery, is standing ironing her wedding outfit while she's wearing it.* DERIC *runs in, rummages for the tin of black shoe polish, and starts out again.*

MOTHER   Ten minutes of this rain'll do more good in half an hour than a fortnight of ordinary rain would do in a month.

DERIC *stops dead; stares at her. A beat.*

DERIC   There is no rain.

MOTHER   That apart.

A little later the BEST MAN *is leaning against his car, a piece of paper in his hand, trying to memorise his speech.*

BEST MAN   And finally, I'd just like to thank . . . *(checks his notes)* . . . Jill and Myrna for helping with the delicate work on the bridesmaids' dresses . . . *(checks his notes)* . . . and my sister Sandra for not helping . . .

Out of the door, in their wedding clothes, come SALLY, NICK *and* DERIC'S MOTHER – *followed by* DERIC *wheeling* DIANA. *The wheelchair is garlanded with silk flowers and streamers; and* DIANA, *radiant and beautiful with happiness and excitement, is wearing her red hat.* DERIC *wheels her to the Citroën. The* NEIGHBOURS *watch – one or two of them near to tears.*

43 Church

DERIC *helps* DIANA *out of her wheelchair and into the church.*

DIANA   I'm not saying that . . . It's not my wedding, love, it's hers.

DERIC   You're still entitled to walk down the aisle.

DIANA   Not if I don't get there until the christening!

Inside the ORGANIST *is playing a warm-up hymn. The main door of the church creaks back.* DERIC *helps* DIANA *in. He supports her from behind, with his arms under hers. They move a few shuffling steps.*

DIANA   Right, where's the starting line?

DERIC   Here, level with the first pew.

They continue their sand-dance.

DERIC   You don't have to do this you know?

She looks at him as though he's barmy. He relents. DIANA *begins one slow, shuffling step after another. If she fails,* DERIC'S *arm is only centimetres behind her.*

DIANA   If it looks like I'm going to crack it, give the kids a shout, will you love?

But NICK *and* SALLY *have already come inside the church, along with a handful of close friends. They are watching from the doorway. The* ORGANIST *is now in full swing and keeping a watchful eye on the proceedings.*

The pain shows on DIANA'S *face. One foot moves forward. She bites her lower lip, to goad the second one alongside. Her progress is very slow, but it is progress. She falters once, and it looks like she's going to fall.* DERIC'S *arm quickly moves to catch her, but she recovers her balance.*

DIANA   I'm okay. *(pause)* Halfway yet?

DERIC   Do you want to stop for a breather?

DIANA   *(in pain)* . . . No . . . no. *(pointing to her legs and in stage whisper)* Once these get a sniff of a sit-down, that'll be it.

DERIC   Would you like me to . . . ?

DIANA   *(kindly)* Shut up. *(looking at him)* Please, love. I'm a bit like Rocky, I can't walk and talk at the same time.

DIANA *shuffles her way towards the front pew. Close-up on her face as she hums along with the organ, despite her frustration and pain. Unseen by her the congregation is filling up the church from the back. The rousing music is drowning out the odd cough and moaning infant. The vicar watches from the vestry as he adjusts his robes. There isn't a single person in the church who isn't willing her to succeed.*

DIANA *trembles with the effort. There are only four more pews to the front. Her strength is ebbing away fast.* DERIC *whispers something to her, but she waves him away. She steadies herself on the end of the third pew, closing her eyes for a moment, overcome by the effort.*

She looks up to see NICK *and* SALLY *standing by the front pew.*
NICK *puts out his hand.*

SALLY   Just fall over, Mum, you'll still make it.

The organ music is reaching its climax.

DIANA   *(forcing a smile, hardly able to speak)* This bloody shoe's killing me!

DIANA'S *legs grudgingly take her the last few steps to her son's hand. He puts his arm round her and gently lowers her on to the front pew.*

NICK   *(into her ear)* Thanks, mum.

First one shout of 'Well done, Diana' cuts through the crescendo of music, then another. DIANA *turns to see that the church has filled to bursting with her family and friends. The whole congregation bursts into spontaneous applause.*
  The ORGANIST *catches sight of the bride entering the church and unleashes the 'Wedding March'. The congregation falls silent.*

44 Wedding reception

A three-piece band plays. GUESTS *are eating at a buffet, drinking, chatting, laughing. On the dance floor, couples are dancing. Among them, miraculously, are* DERIC *and* DIANA. *Miraculously, that is, until a low-angle shot reveals* DERIC *is holding* DIANA *upright – and her feet are standing on his. They 'dance' past* DERIC'S MOTHER *who is engaged in conversation with a* GUEST.

GUEST   Are you Deric's mother or Diana's?

MOTHER   *(thrown)* Um . . . *(tries to work it out)* Um . . . *(brightens)* Deric's father.

DERIC *and* DIANA *'dance' on. We've never seen them so happy.*

DIANA   My hat was a triumph.

DERIC   So were you.

DIANA   Can I wear it at my funeral?

DERIC'S *smile fades.*

DIANA   Say yes.

Tears start into DERIC'S *eyes. The band plays on; the guests laugh and chatter.* DERIC *nods 'yes' to her question.*

45 Hospital for Nervous Diseases, London – Night

It is three months later. An old, tattered METHS DRINKER *is sprawled, swigging at a bottle, at the front of the steps leading up to the entrance of the hospital.* DERIC *comes out of the door, pulling a packet of cigarettes and a lighter from his pocket. He leans against the door post and lights a cigarette. The* METHS DRINKER *offers him his bottle.*

METHS DRINKER   Want a swig?

DERIC *smiles and shakes his head.*

METHS DRINKER   I used to live in Coventry until a year ago. *(long pause)* But I thought, sod it, I thought, I'll come down to London. That's where the opportunities are. *(long pause)* What's your story?

DERIC   Me? Oh . . . I came down to see my wife.

METHS DRINKER   Try the Embankment. It's full of the bitches.

DERIC   She's in here.

He nods towards the hospital. The METHS DRINKER *follows his glance, then looks back at* DERIC, *uncomprehending.*

DERIC   We went to a wedding three months ago, and she's had to have a lie-down . . . ever since.

METHS DRINKER   Bitches, all of them. *(looking at* DERIC'S *cigarette)* Gi's a drag.

DERIC *gives him what's left of his cigarette and goes back into the hospital.*

Inside illuminated bleakly by the night-lights, DIANA *is lying in bed, her eyes closed.* DERIC *is seated beside her, watching her worriedly. After a few moments . . .*

DIANA   *(her voice very weak)* Aileen phoned me.

DERIC   How is she?

DIANA   She's going to Chichester for the weekend.

DERIC   Yeah. Writers' conference.

DIANA   She said you'd been invited as well, but said no.

DERIC   I've a previous engagement – I promised myself I'd defrost the fridge.

DIANA *smiles. She opens her eyes and takes his hand.*

DIANA   You go, love. Aileen'll be there.

He looks at her, searching her eyes. His are confused; hers, serene.

DERIC   What are you saying?

DIANA   *(a small laugh)* I'm saying go to Chichester, love. Don't look so worried. *(nods towards the bedside locker)* There's a little present in there for her. In Christmas wrapping. I know it's not Christmas . . . but, then again . . . when is it ever?

DERIC *opens the locker and brings out a small packet wrapped in Christmas paper. He gently squeezes* DIANA'S *hand.*

46 Exterior of hotel in Chichester

DERIC *and* AILEEN *are seated at one of the tables on a verandah, having tea.* DERIC *hands the parcel to* AILEEN. *She opens it – and brings out the bikini which we saw in the Longdens' bedroom earlier. She feels it.* DERIC'S *heart somersaults.*

AILEEN   What is it? *(no response)* Deric?

DERIC   *(quietly)* A brand-new bikini she's had six years. *(removing a letter attached to it)* And a letter.

AILEEN   Read it.

DERIC   *(reads)* 'Dear buggerlugs, I hope you've a swimming pool in the hotel. Randy Longden here bought it for me at Coles in Sheffield a couple of lifetimes ago. The girl in the shop said it'd fit me like a second skin. Which is why I want you to have it. To be my second skin. *(pause)* I'm discharging myself from the hospital as soon as I'm fit to travel. The consultant finally told me the only cure is to accept that there isn't one, and stop fighting it. *(pause)* Sorry if the writing's a bit wobbly only I'm dictating it to nurse from Sierra Leone and she's having trouble with her boyfriend. Now put your bikini on and let Deric chuck you in the deep end. Love, Diana.'

A long pause. AILEEN *takes* DERIC'S *hand.*

DERIC   Why 'second skin'?

AILEEN   I've a confession to make, love.

DERIC   What's she mean, 'second skin'?

AILEEN   We both have a confession to make. Me and Diana.

DERIC Am I up to it?

AILEEN I shouldn't think so, no.

AILEEN *takes a deep breath. This isn't going to be easy.*

AILEEN Diana and I have a little secret you were never supposed to know.

DERIC She knew I'd be reading this . . .

AILEEN What she wants is for you to fall in love with me.

A long pause. DERIC *is close to tears.*

DERIC I don't think I can love anyone more than I love her.

AILEEN She knows that. So do I.

DERIC She won't die. I won't let her.

AILEEN Well, I think that's probably what she's banking on. Was banking on . . .

She picks up the bikini and feels it.

AILEEN   . . . till now.

47 The Longdens' house

DIANA *is in bed.* DERIC, *in his pyjamas, crosses from the window and puts on his dressing gown.*

DERIC Beautiful day outside.

DIANA It's not so good in here . . . I've got pins and needles in one of my legs and I can't tell which . . .

DERIC *starts rummaging under her bedclothes.*

DIANA Are you interfering with me, I hope?

He produces a hot water bottle, with a magician's flourish, from inside the bed.

DERIC Ta-ra!! *(feels it)* Cold as ice . . . I'll bring you a hot one.

DIANA Cold? It felt boiling to me. Can I have another bath, love, as well? I'm sorry . . . must be the umpteenth . . .

DERIC Who's counting?

He goes.

In the bathroom the hot water from the tap pours into the rapidly filling steam bath. DERIC *pours bath salts into it. Then he takes dry towels from the airing cupboard and puts them by the bath, picks up the wet towels from the floor and the rail, turns off the tap and exits.*

DIANA *in bed, as before.* DERIC *comes in, the wet towels over his arm.*

DERIC Okay, love. All ready.

DIANA In a minute . . . something hurts when I move. I'm not sure what.

DERIC No hurry. I'll stick these in the washer.

He goes out again.

A few moments later, in the kitchen, DERIC *is putting the wet towels and other items of dirty washing, including oven gloves, into the washing machine. He switches it on, then goes to a boiling kettle and starts re-filling the hot water bottle.*

DERIC *(calling)* I reckon Sally wears the oven gloves on her feet to do the gardening in. Oven boots. Hey, how about that? You could wear them on your feet in bed – or stick your feet in the oven. Ve haf vays of making you varm! What d'you think?

During the course of his babbling, a gut feeling of shadowy apprehension is beginning to grip him.

DERIC   On the other hand, don't mention it to my mother. My dad once gave her a pair of oven gloves for Christmas. She said her oven didn't need them – you just switched it on and it warmed up on its own. But that was in the days when she spoke English.

In the bedroom, a few moments later, DERIC *comes in with the hot water bottle. The bed's empty.*

DERIC   *(calls)* Mrs Longden?

He puts the hot water bottle in the bed and goes out again.

DERIC *pops his head around the toilet door. The room is empty.*

DERIC   Diana?

He goes out again.

DERIC *pushes open the bathroom door.* DIANA, *in her nightdress, is face down in the bath, one foot curled over the rim, her hair swimming.*

   DERIC *leaps forward, puts his arm under her and tries to lift her out. Her body jack-knifes and slides out of his grasp. Frantically, he yanks her head above the water. Still holding her, he jumps into the bath and tries to heave her out. She won't move. He slips down into the water, and tries to lever her out with his knee and arms. She still doesn't move. He stands up and tugs at her with all his strength – and still can't raise her.*

DERIC   Please! Diana!

He moves his foot and finally manages to lift her out of the bath and on to the floor. She's dead. Kneeling beside her, he pumps her body, presses her, tries the kiss of life . . .

DERIC   I was standing on your hand. I couldn't get you out . . . I was standing on your bloody hand . . .!

Weeping helplessly, he hugs her to him, stroking her wringing hair.

In the hallway DERIC *phones 999; wet through, sobbing.*

DERIC   Ambulance, quick. *(beat; gives his address)* She's dead . . . I think she's drowned . . . She has blackouts . . . had . . . had blackouts.

He puts the phone down . . . and the doorbell rings. DERIC *drags himself to the door and opens it. Two* MEN *in suits and carrying briefcases are there.*

1ST MAN   Mr Deric Longden?

DERIC   She's upstairs.

1ST MAN   We're Customs and Excise.

DERIC   Sorry?

2ND MAN   To inspect your VAT returns. You had a letter.

DERIC   Go away. Please go away.

2ND MAN   *(smiles knowingly)* With your accountant, are they?

DERIC *closes the door on the* MEN.

48 Crematorium

The room is jam-packed with virtually everybody we've seen who knows the Longdens . . . FRED *of 'Fred's hands' fame, the* RECEPTIONIST *from Hallamshire Hospital, the* POSTMAN, NICK'S BRIDE *and her family, his* BEST MAN *and the wedding guests,* JOAN, SHEILA, *and all the girls from the factory, the* CHEMIST, 'KENNETH OF ARABIA', MINNIE BONSALL *and* DOCTOR ROPER. DERIC, SALLY, NICK *and* DERIC'S MOTHER *stand at the front. The* MINISTER *faces them.*

MINISTER   Deric made Diana a promise. She wanted the pop song 'Wide-Eyed and Legless' played at her funeral. She thought it appropriate since she spent half her time in a wheelchair and still, ratherly cleverly she thought, managed to fall downstairs the other half . . .

An organ begins playing 'Wide-Eyed and Legless'.

MINISTER   He made her another promise. She's wearing it now.

We see for the first time, the coffin, with DIANA'S *red hat perched upon it.*

MINISTER   Those of us who knew Diana in the years before she ever sat in a wheelchair, know she didn't sit down at all. She just didn't walk.

Outside scores and scores of mourners stand, heads bowed, listening to the tannoy. Among them, to one side, is AILEEN, *holding a flower.*

MINISTER   She ran. She ran through life – laughing – making other people laugh. And she did it with a love of life. Loving – and making other people love.

Inside, the coffin, with the red hat on it, travels through the curtain towards the incinerator, and out of sight.

Outside, DERIC *and his family are gently besieged by friends comforting them, as they make their way slowly to the Citroën.* SALLY *is particularly distraught.* MOTHER *is talking to a small group.*

MOTHER   Mrs Gandhi popped her clogs in India. I used to like her dad. He got an Oscar. And now Rock Hudson's popped his. It's funny – the one person I never thought'd pop her clogs . . . was Diana.

DERIC, NICK *and* SALLY *walk towards the car. They are surrounded by the mourners from both inside the building and out.*

DERIC She once asked me did I think many people'd turn up for her funeral.

He walks over to AILEEN, *who is standing alone.*

DERIC Only me.

AILEEN I know.

They join SALLY *and* NICK *at the car.*

NICK Thanks, Aileen.

AILEEN What for?

SALLY For writing the minister's speech for him. It was beautiful. Mum'd have loved it.

AILEEN She lived it, Sally. Writing it was a doddle.

DERIC *opens the driver's door and is about to get in when he notices* SALLY *and* NICK *very deliberately shepherding* AILEEN *towards the front passenger door.* AILEEN *hesitates as though she has no right . . . but they're gently insistent. They settle* AILEEN *in the seat beside* DERIC – *and share a sad, half-smile with him as he watches. Then they get in the back on either side of* DERIC'S MOTHER. *The car drives off.*

49 Country road

The Citroën is driving along, between rolling fields. Over this, we hear:

MOTHER'S VOICE I had a stand-up wash before I came out. 'Well,' I thought, 'life has to go on . . . ' *(pause)* I remember when this was all fields . . .

The car drives into the distance.

Glossary: reading the text

Scenes 1–6

1. *Matlock, Derbyshire*   market town situated south of Sheffield in the Derbyshire Dales.

   nasal inhaler   plastic tube containing decongestent: breathed in, it clears the nose during heavy colds.

   yanked out   (slang) pulled out violently.

2. *Citroën Safari*   French-built car; Safari is the model.

3. *Hallamshire Hospital*   the Royal Hallamshire Hospital, Sheffield.

4. *Arnold Schwarzenegger*   film-star, famous for his large physique and tough action films.

   Neurological   relating to the nervous system.

   Renal   relating to the kidneys.

5. *summat*   (slang) something.

   Prince Charming   in the fairy tale, Cinderella is saved from a life of drudgery by the prince.

   ineffectually   without success.

6. *chuck*   (slang) term of affection, like 'dear'.

   beat   a stage direction used by Jack Rosenthal to indicate a very brief pause.

7. *appraises*   estimates their quality.

   lurches   moves abruptly.

   Palookaville   (US slang) an out-of-the-way, slow town; a place where nothing happens.

8. *Intercut*   switch rapidly to and from.

   sec   second.

GLOSSARY

9 *the 'Titanic'* the 'unsinkable' luxury liner which collided with an iceberg in the North Atlantic in 1912; 1,513 passengers drowned.

bemusedly in a puzzled manner.

biopsy medical examination of human tissue.

paralysed unable to feel or move.

10 *Moron* (slang) idiot.

11 *She magazine* popular women's magazine containing fashion items, short stories and general interest features.

Morecambe Lancashire seaside resort.

12 *Lateral thinking* considering ideas from an unusual or 'sideways' viewpoint.

13 *literary lunch* meal arranged for a group of writers.

flogging (slang) selling.

Buick American make of car.

15 *popped his clogs* (slang) died.

Count Basie American jazz bandleader and composer, born 1904.

Johnny Weissmuller Olympic swimming champion who became famous for his film portrayal of Tarzan.

---

1 What are your impressions so far of the characters of Deric and Diana?

2 What have you learnt about their relationship? What do they have in common? What does each gain from the other?

3 What impression have you gained of the medical pofession?

Scenes 7–14

17 *Chesterfield* industrial town in Derbyshire.

spruce neat.

GLOSSARY

19 *'Three Nuns'*   a brand of tobacco.

20 *nowt*   (northern dialect) nothing.

    Kojak   TV detective of the 1970s, famous for his completely bald head.

21 *tentatively*   nervously.

    mistletoe   evergreen plant traditionally used at Christmas to kiss beneath.

22 *Poofter*   (slang) derogatory term meaning homosexual.

23 *Directory Enquiries*   telephone service which provides enquirers with telephone numbers.

27 *skedaddle*   (colloquial) hurry away.

    Stafford Cripps   British Labour politician (1889–1952).

28 *suburban*   residential area on the outskirts of a town or city.

    Someone of Arabia   confused reference to David Lean's epic film, *Lawrence of Arabia*.

29 *Richard Burton...James Mason*   British stage and film actors.

30 *croupier*   person who collects bets and pays winnings at a gambling table.

---

1 What have we learnt so far about the Longdens' children? How do they react to their mother's illness?

2 How would you describe Deric's mother? What is her role in the screenplay – is it for comic relief? Or does her humour serve a more serious purpose?

3 What is the importance of Deric's 'other lives' – his factory and his freelance writing? What part do they play in his life?

Scenes 15–31

32 *bridle*   become irritated.

33 *Hysteria*   a mental condition characterised by highly emotional outbursts and paralysis.

35 *Dante's Inferno*   an epic poem by Italian writer Dante Alighieri (1265–1321) describing a journey through hell.

37 *The VAT*   a shortened way of referring to the tax inspectors who check businesses' value added tax records.

40 *faux pas*   (French) error – literally, a false step.

42 *skirmish*   small-scale fight.

Happy Families   a card game.

43 *mêlee*   crowd.

gobsmacked   (northern slang) shocked; speechless.

Lycra body-stockings   one-piece outfit made from thin stretch-fabric.

MAITRE D'   head waiter.

44 *fatuous*   empty.

dolloped   (colloquial) served a semi-solid lump.

45 *Bon appetite*   (French) phrase to wish someone an enjoyable meal. Here, the English spelling of 'appetite' emphasises that the words are pronounced with a definite English accent.

46 *innocuous*   innocent, harmless.

48 *boggle*   show confusion.

51 *burbling*   talking quickly and unclearly.

52 *millinery*   hats.

53 *euphoric*   full of high spirits.

55 *maniacally*   like a mad person.

A stitch in time   A reference to the proverb 'A stitch in time saves nine' – a small correction early on can save large problems later.

GLOSSARY

63 *chiropodist*   someone who specialies in the treatment of minor foot problems.

64 *Welsh rarebits*   grilled cheese on toast.

> 1 What does Deric like and admire about Aileen Armitage?
> 2 What does Diana's attitude to Aileen reveal about her own character and her love for Deric?
> 3 How have the characters of Diana and Deric changed during the screenplay so far?

Scenes 32–49

66 *barmy*   (colloquial) mad.

King's Cross   railway station in London serving trains to and from the north of England.

Soho   district of London known for its striptease joints and prostitution.

bravado   outward self-confidence.

67 *orderly*   hospital attendant.

convulsion   violent muscle spasm.

71 *judicious*   sensible.

74 *convalescence*   total rest, usually following illness.

75 *traipsing*   (colloquial) walking wearily.

volition   choice.

76 *dab hand*   (colloquial) skilful.

77 *run a gauntlet*   expose themselves to criticism.

79 *yanks off*   (slang) pulls off.

81 *Rocky*   film character of a boxer, played by Sylvester Stallone.

GLOSSARY

83 *the Embankment*   the area bordering the River Thames in London, where a lot of homeless people congregate.

87 *flourish*   dramatic movement.

umpteenth   (colloquial) latest of many.

90 *Mrs Gandhi*   Indira Ghandi (1917–84), twice Indian Prime Minister.

Oscar   award presented annually by the Academy of Motion Picture Arts and Science in the USA for outstanding achievements in film-making. Deric's mother is referring to the film, *Gandhi*.

Rock Hudson   US film actor.

---

1   Why is Nick's wedding so important to Diana?

2   Even at the saddest moment in the screenplay, Deric's mother has comical lines. What effect does this have on your response to the final scenes?

3   What is your final impression of Diana? Her suffering? Her sense of humour? Her attitude to Aileen? Choose a moment from the play which you think best captures her personality.

Study programme

Characters

Diana

1. Make a spider diagram to show the different sides of Diana's character – for example, her humour, determination, etc. Discuss which of these you think is most important in the play.

2. Design a graph to trace Diana's and Deric's emotional development during the play. Along the lower axis show key events from the screenplay (e.g. first visit to hospital, journey on the train to London, removal of the last five pages from her file, purchase of the red hat, etc.) and on the vertical axis the characters' emotional state.

   Do their moments of joy and despair match – or does one character's emotions serve as a contrast to the other's?

3. Write a monologue as Diana looking back over her life immediately prior to contracting ME and contrasting it with the period of the disease itself.

   Consider the positive as well as the negative aspects of her experience of this illness.

4. Write Diana's diary entry after Deric has confronted her with the bottle of Soneral sleeping tablets in scene 19. Look carefully at this part of the text, including her reaction to the news that Nick is about to be married.

   Remember that Diana uses humour as a way of escaping the pain of the present.

STUDY PROGRAMME

Look for other examples which show Diana and Deric's strong understanding of one another.

7 When Deric is with Aileen he uses the time to talk about Diana. In fact, when it seems as though their relationship is about to develop Aileen diffuses the situation, taking him for a walk, so that he can tell her all about Diana. Deric feels relieved as though a burden has been momentarily removed from his shoulders.

Why does he feel like this and why does he use this precious time for himself to discuss Diana?

8 Considering Deric's public persona – of a man who is juggling his factory, writing and caring for his wife, yet able to cope – why does he crash his car and what significance does this have?

Look closely at the thoughts he has which lead up to the accident. Using a similar style and with the objective of reflecting Deric's private exhaustion, frustration and sadness, write his thoughts as he looks at himself shaving in the mirror before seeing to Diana's breakfast and the full day before him.

9 Add a scene to the play that would come after one of Deric and Diana's many visits to the hospital.

Aim to bring out their way of coping with others' ignorance, their pain and lack of hope. Remember how important humour is to their characters. You should also show the conflicts of the two. Diana wants independence but has had it taken away from her. Deric is 'outwardly calm, inwardly weighed down'.

Mother

1 What does the inclusion of Deric's mother add to the story? Look back to what he has to say about her in 'The writer on writing' on page xii.

STUDY PROGRAMME

Describe her character, with reference to the text, commenting on whether she just provides relief from the pain and hopelessness of Diana's condition or whether you feel that we have something to learn from her. Does she perhaps prevent Deric from being too aware of his own problems or is she an additional burden on his emotional resources?

2. In *Lost for Words*, Deric Longden writes about his mother. She has a stroke which affects the part of her brain responsible for speech. His mother becomes frustrated by the fact that conversation has been taken away from her and that she can no longer make herself understood.

Write a monologue as if you are Deric's mother looking back on your life, the people you know, Diana's illness, your cat, Whisky, and your son, Deric.

Perform this monologue as though you are speaking her trapped thoughts for her.

3. After his mother's first stroke, Deric wants her to move in with him but she refuses. Search for evidence in the text which you feel would have caused you to predict this response.

Sally and Nick

1. After Diana's death, Sally and Nick are invited to speak in a radio programme devoted to the subject of ME. The presenter wants to establish facts about the disease first, in order to inform his/her audience. He then asks more personal questions about seeing their parents coping with the situation, to find out how the family dealt with such a trauma. Aim to perform the result.

2. How do you feel Sally and Nick are influenced by the strong characters of their parents?

STUDY PROGRAMME

Examine the parts of the text where they appear, considering in what ways both characters compare and contrast with Deric and Diana.

3 As Diana walks down the aisle on Nick's wedding day, both Nick and Sally watch her progress in silence, willing her to succeed.

Read scene 43 through again and then as either Sally or Nick write your thoughts as you watch your mother painfully and slowly make her way towards the front of the church.

4 You are either Sally or Nick and have decided to write a book about your experience of Diana's ME and suffering. Write the opening chapter with a synopsis of the rest. It should be 1,500-2,000 words long and include comment about your feelings, any humour in the situation, ME, the ignorance of those around you, the courage of your parents and the sleeping pills.

Aim for realism rather than melodrama.

Aileen

1 Aileen and Diana become friends when we might have expected them to be rivals. Describe their motives and what this friendship suggests about their individual characters.

2 When Deric agrees to take Diana to see Aileen in scene 41, he is 'bewildered' by the sound of their laughter which he can hear coming from the living room. It occurs to him that they sound like 'two old friends'.

Write a script of their conversation and perform it, using parts of the dialogue that are already given. Consider the situation carefully, remembering that while Aileen shares Diana's strength and sense of humour, this is still a difficult situation for both of them.

3 Write a diary entry as Aileen reflecting back over the literary luncheon where you first met Deric. Read scene 20 again carefully before you start in order to select the relevant information.

Your writing should be informative as well as attempting to convey Aileen's sense of humour and sensitivity.

4 Deric Longden married Aileen in 1989. Imagine that you are Aileen at this time. Write an account of your life from the moment you first met Deric, tracing your contact and friendship with Diana and finishing with your present situation.

Aileen's main focus should be the influence that both Deric and Diana Longden have had over her life.

5 What do you think is the importance of Aileen in the play? Does her presence add anything to our understanding of Diana and/or Deric Longden?

Themes

The medical profession

1 What impression do we receive of the medical profession in the play? Examine the text closely and support your findings with specific examples.

2 Write a doctor's report on Diana commenting on the 'hysteria' you believe she is experiencing, which is the cause of her having blackouts.

The language of this report should be formal and informative and the tone dismissive. Comment on her behaviour rather than trying to get to the root of the illness.

STUDY PROGRAMME

3 Why does the question 'how are her periods?' (page 10) make Diana so angry? What does it reveal about the attitude of the doctor to Diana's illness?

4 Doctor Roper remarks to Deric that he is rather an 'anxious husband' (page 31). What criticism is implied in this statement? Why is Deric thought to be over-anxious?

5 For what reasons does Doctor Roper hand Diana her file to take back to the front desk (page 34)? What does this mean to Diana?

6 Imagine you are Doctor Roper. Write a detailed account of her meeting with Diana and Deric Longden in scene 16 which she relays to a close and trusted fellow doctor. Include comment on the difficulty she experiences in judgement between her professionalism and personal sense of justice.

7 How and why does the medical profession fail Diana?

8 Why do Deric and Diana have to face ignorance in their struggle against ME? What is the ignorance they face? Why does it exist?

How do you feel one should fight such ignorance? Why is it dangerous?

9 During Diana's visits to hospitals she experiences a depressing quality in the response of the doctors to her illness. She declares that at first they are intrigued and want answer but after a short while, when it becomes clear that answers are elusive, they lose interest. Why does this happen? What does this response indicate?

Illness and suffering

1 Pain can be experienced both mentally as well as physically. Who suffers pain in the play? Give details of the type that each particular character experiences, and at what moments.

Is the character's way of coping with the pain the same for both types? Explain your answer with reference to the text.

2 Deric experiences private anguish and despair. Why does he not attempt to share this with his wife? What effect does keeping it private have upon his state of mind? Do you think it helps his situation to keep things in like this?

3 Diana and Deric's relationship is a unit built to withstand the ignorance of the outside world. Why do they have to do this? What pain do they still have to face and what do they manage to avoid?

4 How has Aileen managed to cope with the pain of an unsuccessful and unhappy marriage coupled with the fact that she is blind? Is this what draws her and Deric together? Have they a common bond in pain?

Humour

1 What do Deric and Diana use humour for? Choose two examples from the play where humour is apparent in their conversation and explain how it is used and what implications we can draw from its presence.

Is there any possible danger in their use of humour to avoid despair?

2 Think about the type of humour used by the Longdens. Should actors playing the parts laugh at the humour, or treat it seriously?

3 Write an additional scene to be added to the play. Your scene would come directly after scene 41, when Deric and Diana have been to visit Aileen. They are sitting in their living room discussing the afternoon they have had.

Aim to bring out their use of humour and the strength of their relationship. Think about the conflicting private emotions that both will be experiencing and include comment on these in stage directions.

4. What does Deric's mother add to the humour of the play? How important is this for the audience, do you think?

5. Does the way in which Deric and his wife often communicate with each other (i.e. through humour) indicate that their relationship is weak, based on pretence, or strong, founded on complete understanding?

Choose examples from the text to provide evidence for your answer and explain your reasoning.

Structure and language

1. Write your own introduction to feature at the beginning of the play. Comment on the opening scene in order to provide a context for Diana's illness and Deric's predicament.

You should provide factual information about ME as well as about the family. Include personal comments about Deric and Diana's relationship.

2. You have been asked to write a synopsis, to accompany the video, on the background of the Longdens, ME and about the content of the play in general.

It is to be 500-1,000 words and should be informative, aimed at 15-16-year-olds.

STUDY PROGRAMME

3 What effect is Jack Rosenthal trying to achieve by having short scenes that rapidly change to different situations with different characters? How is this structure different from a stage play?

4 Thinking particularly about Diana and Deric, what do we learn of their characters and feelings through the stage directions?

Select two examples for each and compare them to what is revealed through their speech. Comment on what similarities and differences you can find.

5 Read through the first three scenes again. Imagine that you are Deric Longden and that the content of these first three scenes is to be that of the first chapter of your book about Diana. Write this chapter, thinking carefully about the style Deric would adopt. (Look back to 'The writer on writing' on page v for clues.)

In a commentary on this task, explain what changes had to be made in adapting the screenplay to fit the style and structure of a book. How is your final result different from your source material?

6 Imagine that the end of the play includes a scene in the Longden's living room, where Deric, Sally, Nick, Deric's mother and Aileen are all present.

Write this scene concentrating on the different characters present. Aim to bring out their differences but also their similarities. Their conversation should be tinged with humour and understanding, but also with grief and sadness.

Study questions

Many of the activities you have already completed will help you to answer the following questions. Before you begin to write, consider these points about essay writing:

STUDY PROGRAMME

- Analyse what the question is asking. Do this by circling key words or phrases and numbering each part.
- Use each part of the question to 'brainstorm' ideas and references to the novel which you think are relevant to the answer.
- Decide on the order in which you are going to tackle the parts of the question. It may help you to draw a flow-diagram of the parts so that you can see which aspects of the question are linked.
- Organise your ideas and quotations into sections to fit your flow-diagram. You can do this by placing notes in columns under the various headings.
- Write a first draft of your essay. Do not concern yourself too much with paragraphing and so on; just aim to get your ideas down on paper and do not be too critical of what you write.
- Redraft as many times as you need, ensuring all the time that:
  - each paragraph addresses the questions;
  - each paragraph addresses a new part of the question, or at least develops a part;
  - you have an opening and closing paragraph which are clear and linked to the question set;
  - you have checked for spelling and other grammatical errors.

[1] Write a detailed comparison of Diana and Deric.
- What attitudes and qualities do they have in common?
- What differences are there in their attitudes?
- How do they help one another to cope with the stresses of Diana's illness?
- How do they develop during the play?

[2] Discuss the importance of humour in the play. Think about:
- how humour helps the characters to cope with the traumas of the illness;
- how it shapes our sympathies towards the characters;
- how it creates contrasts within the screenplay, emphasising the tragedy of Diana's situation.

STUDY PROGRAMME

Finally, discuss whether you think there are any moments when the humour included is inappropriate.

3. How has the screenplay changed your attitude to illness? Consider:
   - the facts you have learnt about ME;
   - the way Jack Rosenthal shows the characters responding to the illness;
   - the impact on family life such an illness can have;
   - the conclusion of the play.

4. What are the key moments from the screenplay in each character's life? Choose one moment each for Diana and Deric and write about how this incident or event affects them. You might choose to write in role.

5. Write about the role played by the minor characters in the screenplay – for example, Deric's mother, Nick and Sally.
   - How do they react to Diana's illness?
   - What different attitudes do they show?
   - What is the importance in the screenplay of 'family'?

6. Discuss Aileen's part in the screenplay. Why is she important both to Diana and to Deric? Discuss what qualities she brings out in each character.

7. Write an analysis of the role that the medical profession adopts in the screenplay. Consider:
   - how far you feel it represents both the cause and the enemy of Diana's strength;
   - what Diana is fighting against.

Suggestions for further reading

Diana's Story and ***Lost for Words*** by Deric Longden
These books tell the story of ***Wide-Eyed and Legless***, describing the writer's life with Diana, his mother and his children. They illuminate the screenplay, adding detail about what happened to the family and give a rich, often humorous, picture of the way the Longdens coped with Diana's illness.

Have the Men had Enough? by Margaret Forster
A family has to cope with their grandmother as her mind rapidly gives way. As she becomes increasingly unable to survive alone, other options must be looked at – many of them showing with bitterness the limitations of the State's capacity to care.

Children of a Lesser God by Mark Medoff
When James, a speech teacher, begins work at a school for the deaf, he becomes intrigued by Sarah. In her mid-twenties, deaf from birth, she stubbornly refuses to lip-read or accept help. A love story, the play also illuminates the pride and independence of its deaf characters, juxtaposing their creativity against the stifling ethos of the school.

A Day in the Life of Joe Egg by Peter Nichols
Bri and Sheila's daughter (Joe) is born with damage to the cerebral cortex, making her 'a vegetable'. The couple's ability to cope is severely tested, sinking at times to despair. This play tackles difficult emotional issues in a mode of dark comedy that has left many audiences disturbed and upset.

Awakenings by Oliver Sacks
Twenty of Dr Sacks' patients suffer from a mysterious illness, an epidemic of sleeping-sickness which put them asleep in the 1920s. Now, forty years later, he uses the drug L-DOPA to bring them briefly back to the real world. A fascinating study, made into a film starring Robin Williams and Robert de Niro.

Wider reading assignments

[1] Read Deric Longden's account of his life with Diana and compare it with Jack Rosenthal's screenplay.

What do the different forms (autobiography and screen drama) add to the story? What advantages and disadvantages does each form have? What have you enjoyed about each text? Write a detailed comparison.

[2] Compare two books which deal with humans coping with illness. What strategies do people use to help themselves survive? How do they change in the process?

[3] Compare the screenplays of two films about illness – for example, *Wide-Eyed and Legless*, *Awakenings*, *Children of a Lesser God*, or *Mask*.

Choose two characters who have to cope with traumatic experiences and write a detailed study of the way they are portrayed.

[4] Contrast the humour that you have found in your reading of similar works with that present in Deric Longden's writing. Consider the part humour plays alongside pain and what its function appears to be. Are there similarities in the way humour is used?

Longman Literature
Series editor: Roy Blatchford

Novels

Jane Austen   *Pride and Prejudice*   0 582 07720 6
Charlotte Brontë   *Jane Eyre*   0 582 07719 2
Emily Brontë   *Wuthering Heights*   0 582 07782 6
Anita Brookner   *Hotel du Lac*   0 582 25406 X
Marjorie Darke   *A Question of Courage*   0 582 25395 0
Charles Dickens   *A Christmas Carol*   0 582 23664 9
                 Great Expectations   0 582 07783 4
                 Hard Times   0 582 25407 8
George Eliot   *Silas Marner*   0 582 23662 2
F Scott Fitzgerald   *The Great Gatsby*   0 582 06023 0
                 Tender is the Night   0 582 09716 9
Nadine Gordimer   *July's People*   0 582 06011 7
Graham Greene   *The Captain and the Enemy*   0 582 06024 9
Thomas Hardy   *Far from the Madding Crowd*   0 582 07788 5
                 The Mayor of Casterbridge   0 582 22586 8
                 Tess of the d'Urbervilles   0 582 09715 0
Susan Hill   *The Mist in the Mirror*   0 582 25399 3
Aldous Huxley   *Brave New World*   0 582 06016 8
Robin Jenkins   *The Cone-Gatherers*   0 582 06017 6
Doris Lessing   *The Fifth Child*   0 582 06021 4
Joan Lindsay   *Picnic at Hanging Rock*   0 582 08174 2
Bernard Mac Laverty   *Lamb*   0 582 06557 7
Jan Mark   *The Hillingdon Fox*   0 582 25985 1
Brian Moore   *Lies of Silence*   0 582 08170 X
Beverley Naidoo   *Chain of Fire*   0 582 25403 5
                 Journey to Jo'burg   0 582 25402 7
George Orwell   *Animal Farm*   0 582 06010 9
Alan Paton   *Cry, the Beloved Country*   0 582 07787 7
Ruth Prawer Jhabvala   *Heat and Dust*   0 582 25398 5
Paul Scott   *Staying On*   0 582 07718 4
Virginia Woolf   *To the Lighthouse*   0 582 09714 2

Short stories

Jeffrey Archer   *A Twist in the Tale*   0 582 06022 2
Thomas Hardy   *The Wessex Tales*   0 582 25405 1
Susan Hill   *A Bit of Singing and Dancing*   0 582 09711 8
George Layton   *A Northern Childhood*   0 582 25404 3
Bernard Mac Laverty   *The Bernard Mac Laverty Collection*   0 582 08172 6

Poetry

Five Modern Poets   edited by Barbara Bleiman   0 582 09713 4
Poems from Other Centuries   edited by Adrian Tissier   0 582 22595 X
Poems in My Earphone   collected by John Agard   0 582 22587 6
Poems One   edited by Celeste Flower   0 582 25400 0
Poems Two   edited by Paul Jordan & Julia Markus   0 582 25401 9

Longman Group Limited,
Longman House, Burnt Mill, Harlow,
Essex CM20 2JE, England
and Associated Companies throughout the world.

This edition © Longman Group Limited 1995

Introduction © Deric Longden 1995
Diana's Story © Deric Longden 1989
Lost for Words © Deric Longden 1991
Text of *Wide-Eyed and Legless* © Jack Rosenthal 1995

The right of Jack Rosenthal to be identified as author of *Wide-Eyed and Legless* has been asserted by him in accordance with the Copyright, Design and Patents Act 1988.

All rights reserved; no part of this publication may be reproduced, stored in a retrieval system, or transmitted in any form or by any means, electronic, mechanical, photocopying, recording, or otherwise, without either the prior written permission of the Publishers or a licence permitting restricted copying issued by the Copyright Licensing Agency Ltd, 90 Tottenham Court Road, London W1P 9HE.

This educational edition first published 1995

This play is fully protected by copyright. Rights of performance by amateurs are controlled by the William Morris Agency, 31/32 Soho Square, London W1V 5DG and their permission must be sought before any reading or performance of the play is given.

Editorial material set in 10/12 point Gill Sans Light
Produced by Longman Singapore Publishers (Pte) Ltd
Printed in Singapore

ISBN 0 582 24950 3

Cover illustration by Ramsay Gibb
Cover photograph of Julie Walters © BBC

The publisher's policy is to use paper manufactured from sustainable forests.

Consultants: Geoff Barton and Jackie Head